MW00780597

What others are saying

Paul Gray has put together a winner with "Grace Is..." If you are ready to examine your long held religious views and theology or are already enjoying the life of grace you will find "Grace Is..." full of fresh insight and revelation from an experienced pastor, author, blogger and most importantly seeker of truth.

Dr. Don Keathley
President/Founder Global Grace Seminary, Founding Sr. Pastor
Grace Pointe Community Church, Houston, Tex.

...

Paul Gray with calculatingly quick ease takes a long hidden, barely spoken of and unknown to many, truth...and he brings it into picture-perfect focus for us. This beautiful life changing truth is a spectacular love union between us (all mankind) God the Father, Jesus the Son and The Holy Spirit. But he doesn't stop there, he then shows us that we are included in this love and we have always been included in this love. Paul illustrates to us a beautiful dance we are in. A never-ending dance whose music, choreography and floor is unconditional love, unlimited grace and unending truth. Every word I read expanded my excitement for the next word. Love speaks—no, screams to us-- through this book: "I'm here, I've always been here and I will always be here with you." By the time you finish reading this book you will be undoubtedly sure of God's plan for you and how He feels about you.

Kyle Butler
Pastor and Teacher

As I was reading the book, "Grace Is. . ." by pastor Paul Gray, I kept strongly sensing that I was receiving the most powerful, rich, in-depth, AND practical proclamation of the good news of Jesus Christ I have EVER received.

Through pastor Paul's writing I became ACUTELY AWARE of the union we possess with our Creator, Jesus Christ, our Heavenly Father and the Holy Spirit to a degree I have never known before.

Charles Slagle
Author, Musician

...

It's not often that a "doctrinal" book is a page turner, but very much like Paul's "Convertible Conversations" novel is, so is this book, "Grace Is…"! Whether you believe you know much about grace or whether very little, this is a must read for us all. Unlike many theologians whose writing seems to be meant only for the super educated, Paul Gray writes in such a way that everyone will enjoy and be able to understand. Read on!

Mike Rough
Retired businessman

Dedication

This book is dedicated to all those who have the courage to examine their long-held religious beliefs in the light of Jesus Christ, who is the light of the world. His life defines our lives. In Him, there is no darkness! My hope is that by having the Holy Spirit of Christ reveal to you what Jesus is like, you will then see what God is like. I have experienced that knowing His truth sets us free from any vision of a god that is dark and anything but good. Then we are free indeed! Then we are able to *see what really is!*

Foreword

Marrying the simplicity of the biblical Message with the passion of his own heart, Paul Gray has produced a wonderful handbook that will guide any person into a deeper understanding of the True God who is nothing less than and nothing other than Pure Love. "Grace Is…" is the clear testament of a man who has been set free from a faulty concept and come into the awareness of the Abba whom Jesus came to reveal. With contagious zeal, he brings the reader into that same freedom.

Paul's style is conversational, personal, practical, biblical and powerful. This is a good book to give a friend you wish understood God as you know Him to be. It's an encouragement to the grounded and an evangelistic tool for those still trapped in the calcified, religious paradigm that has enslaved so many people for so long. The chapters blend the simplicity of the historic gospel with the profundity of its Beautiful Truth.

This is a book you will highlight and return to after you've read it. Don't read it too quickly but pause as you go and allow the various facets of the Love that engulfs you to stoke your emotions and stimulate your mind. "Grace Is…" will "take you to church," but not the kind of church you may have attended in the past. This one takes you back to the environment and expression of the early church – the one that proclaimed all inclusive love to the whole world. This is the message that changed the world in the first century and still transforms lives twenty centuries later. Love. That's the message of Jesus Christ and it's presented in all its splendor in these pages.

Dr. Steve McVey
Best-Selling author and Founder of Grace Walk Ministries

Grace Is …

BY PAUL GRAY

Copyright © 2018 by Paul Gray

**MOTIVATION
CHAMPS**
PUBLISHING

ISBN-13: 978-1-7323621-1-6
(Published by God Is for Me, Inc.,/Motivation Champs)

The book was printed in the United States of America. To order additional copies, bulk order, or book speaking engagements contact:
www.gracewithpaulgray.com

Or You May, Contact the Publisher, Motivation Champs Publishing. www.motivationchamps.com

Grace Is …

BY PAUL GRAY

Author of the Amazon #1 Best Seller
Convertible Conversations

Contents

Chapter 1 - God is Love 7

Be Willing to Change Your Mind About Love 8

God Is Love..9

High Love..11

Wide Love..12

Long Love..13

Deep Love 14

No Fear with This Love 15

The Only Thing That Counts...16

Perfect Love 17

God Got Rid of His Record Collection.........................18

Chapter 2 - God is Love in Community.......................... 21

BFFs 22

Loving Relationships 23

Someone to Love...24

First Love...26

Love In Community 27

Fleshing out Community – Part I....................................28

Fleshing out Community – Part II 29

Fleshing out Community – Part III.................................30

Fleshing Out Community – Part IV:
How Did They Do It? 31

Loving and Living in Community....................................32

Chapter 3 - Jesus is Grace 33

Grace Is...34

Jesus Is Grace..36

Resist "But What About …?" 37

Religion's False 'Means of Grace'....................................38

Grace is Many-Faceted..39

The Ability to Respond...40

The Gift of Grace..41

Evil's Goal..42

"That's Not Fair!"...43

Powerfully Unstoppable..44

'Ripped Off' No More 45

Jesus (God) is Full of Grace and Truth 46

Grace is With All Already..47

Not a 'Potential Gift' 48

Who Are You Going To Believe? 49

You Are Attractive! 50

People are Attracted to Christ 52

Restored 54

The Great Conductor..56

Chapter 4 - Glory is God's Grace...61

What Mr. Wiley Was All About 62

Describing God 64

God Describes Himself as 'Grace'...65

God Considers His Glory to Be His Grace.....................................66

Jesus Considers His Glory to Be His Grace....................................68

Christ in You—The Hope of Glory..69

Grace Is With You In Good Times And Bad...................................70

God Gives Grace Through You 71

Jesus Voted For You..72

Grace To You 74

Chapter 5 - Jesus's Finished Work for All Mankind...................77

Good News: Jesus Finished It All 78

Jesus's Finished Work Is All Important..79

Good News: The Cross Was a Success 81

Jesus Did It All—For All 82

All Means All..83

All Really Means All 84

In Christ Before Creation 85

A Completed Victory 87

It's Done and It Lasts Forever 88

It Was All His Doing...89

What Jesus Accomplished In His Finished Work
At The Cross 91

He Glorified You And Sanctified You.....................93

Jesus Reconciled You, Redeemed You and Made You
Friends With God..94

Jesus Totally Took Care of Your Sin Problem And
Made You Right With God!...96

He Set You Free from The Law, Made You His Child,
Chose To Live In You And Never Condemns You 97

God Set You Free And Made You Alive In Christ!
He Has Blessed You 98

He Seated You In Heaven and Gave You
Boldness and Confidence. He Made You Complete.............99

God Accepted You, Gave You Peace and Continues
To Reveal His Grace To YouEvery Day 100

Chapter 6 - Oneness, Union, and Identity............................... 101

The Unseen vs. The Seen Realm 102

The Great Darkness 104

The Teacher Will Show You!................................... 106

The Perceived Darkness of Separation................... 108

Four Circles 110

Radiate Life... 112

Jesus Means That God And Humanity Are Together! 113

Check Your Filter 114

Two Radically Different Ways of Living 115

Christ Is the Unveiling of God's Mystery............... 117

The Nourishment of The Mature 119

Evil's Chief Trick 120

What Do You Do When You Can't See What Is?............... 121

Reality Is Union.. 122

We Have Never Been Apart From God............................. 124

There Is Only One Battle: Union vs. Separation................ 125

Jesus's "I Am" Trumps Evil's "I Am Not" 126

Inseparable Union 127

Corrupt Communion.. 128

Jazz or Classical? 130

Papa's Affirmation To You.. 132

Grace Is the Divine Music Of Life 133

Something Happened.. 134

Your New Standing Negates Your Past............................ 136

You Are Already In 138

It Looks Like 'Unconditional Love' And 'Rest'.................. 139

The Faith Of Jesus 141

Keys To Understanding What Really Is 142

Objective and Subjective... 143

Taking Sides with Jesus 144

Separation Thinking Keeps You In The Dark! 145

'Hell' Comes From The Great Darkness 147

Embracing Union... 148

Mature Spirituality.. 149

The Truth Of All Truths Is Union.................................. 150

Jesus Is Grace and Life Personified!.............................. 152

The Throne of Grace Has Special Meaning for Us! 155

About Paul Gray.. 159

Grace Is ... Action Steps 161

Explanation (*My Message and Assignment*)..................... 163

Books by Paul Gray 167

Paul Gray's Suggested Resources................................ 169

Preface
Have a Convertible Mindset

Things aren't always what they appear to be. You can look at my car (a 2007 Pontiac G6) from a number of different angles—you can even ride in it—and it appears to be a hardtop. You can say, "This car is a hardtop," ... but you'd be mistaken!

I've found that something dramatic usually has to happen for us to change our mind ... to come to see that something's not what we thought it was.

My car is a hardtop convertible; it's capable of being changed. If you weren't familiar with my car, you wouldn't believe it's a convertible because what you see tells you differently.

Convertible means capable of being converted or changed (from one thing to a different thing).

What we think is true, based on information we get from our five senses, may not be true at all! For example, we may look at a person's speech or actions and conclude, "That person is far from God. God will surely punish them forever because they're so bad." We can even believe that about ourselves because of what seems to be obvious to us.

However, God sees things differently. He's not bound by time and space. While appearances may seem to say something to us, He sees what we can't yet see ... what is unseen but true in the eternal realm.

About 2,000 years ago, God appeared to a man named Saul, who had been an extremely religious legalist. Saul was a brilliant religious leader; he was one of the most learned religious leaders in his country ... but most everything he believed was false.

He believed what the religious leaders of his time told him ... never suspecting that their beliefs were built on lies!

He knew about what he *thought* was god, but he didn't know the real God at all.

Jesus personally taught Saul for several years, debunking religion's lies and revealing God's truth to him. Jesus changed his name to Paul and then inspired Paul to pass on these truths to us.

He wrote two thirds of what we call the New Testament, including 2 Corinthians 4:18 (MIRROR): "We are not keeping any score of what seems so obvious to the senses on the surface; it is fleeting and irrelevant; it is the unseen eternal realm within us which has our full attention and captivates our gaze!

"(Until this moment, God remained invisible to mankind; now the authentic begotten Son, the blueprint of mankind's design who represents the innermost being of God, the Son who is in the bosom of the Father, brings Him into full view! He is the official authority qualified to announce God! He is our guide who accurately declares and interprets the invisible God within us.)"

2 Corinthians 3:18 (Parenthesis mine): "The days of window-shopping are over! In Him (Christ) every face is unveiled. In gazing with wonder at the blueprint likeness of God displayed in human form, we suddenly realize that we are looking at ourselves! Every feature of His image is mirrored in us! This is the most radical transformation engineered by the Spirit of the Lord; we are led from an inferior mindset to the revealed endorsement of our authentic identity."

The 'radical transformation' that Paul wrote about is similar to the change in a convertible today. The picture of the top opening up in my car is a great metaphor for our minds being convertible—being able to open up—being open to seeing things that we have never seen before!

When the hardtop is up, nothing from the outside can get in; it can feel safe. But while it may *feel* safe, it's very restricted, limiting and closed off. It's *exclusive*. You're inside, all walled in and protected ... and you're also excluded from what really is! That's a picture of *religion*.

Religion is any attempt to gain or maintain a right relationship with God by our own efforts. Religion fosters judgment, condemnation, shame, exclusivity and generally believes in a fictitious god of our own imaginations ... not Jesus's Papa, the only true God!

Convertible means much more than just a type of car, it means able to change—able to be converted. Then we can *see what really is!*

What really is is wide open, free, glorious—not limited! I can see things I didn't realize were there! I can feel the wind! I can relate to those who are around me.

I've always loved convertibles. I love the freedom, the openness, the ability to relate to my surroundings. And I've become convertible in my beliefs. There's a Greek word that was used a lot 2,000 years ago, 'metanoia.' It means to change your mind, to think differently about something now than you previously thought.

I came to realize that what I thought about a lot of things wasn't true! I needed to be convertible! I needed to change my mind!

I came to the shocking realization that many, actually a*lmost all*, of the things I had believed about God … were not true.

Sadly, a large percentage of what religion teaches is built on lies. We shouldn't be surprised; we have an enemy who is the 'father of lies,' whose name (Diabolos) means deceiver or slanderer. It's actually the Only True God, as Jesus refers to His Father, whom Diabolos slanders, and we are the ones who have been deceived.

Fortunately, the truth about God, which has eluded many, is still true and can be known. God *wants* us to know His truth, and He's in the process of revealing it to people all over the world today!

I grew up going to church every time the doors were open. I continued going faithfully on Sundays as an adult. I tried several different churches in hopes of *finding the right one.*

I heard about who God (supposedly) is, what He's (supposedly) like and what we're (supposed) to do to try to get Him to be merciful with us rather than torture us forever. Each church had a different take on these things … and each was sure *they* were right!

Most religious people, I observed, never questioned those things. I also observed that many of them were uptight, stressed out, becoming burned out and were eventually leaving their churches. They often seemed certain about what they believed … but were miserable. Many of them seemed to walk on eggshells.

At the same time, I observed a large segment of society that didn't believe in an angry, punitive, impossible-to-please deity ... and *they* seemed happier and more able to enjoy life!

I came to realize that the religious people and I, too, had a 'hardtop spiritual mentality'—that I needed to put the top down and be willing to change, to be convertible. I started on an amazing journey that literally gets better every day ... because I now realize every day that God is not like I used to believe.

A more familiar translation of 2 Corinthians 4:18 says, "We do not look at the things which are seen, but at the things which are not seen. For the things which are seen are temporary, but the things which are not seen are eternal."

The Apostle Paul also wrote in 1 Corinthians 2:9, "Eye has not seen, nor ear heard, nor have entered into the heart of man the things which God has prepared for those who love Him."

What you may not have seen or heard, but are about to, is that God has not only prepared, but He has already *given* you grace and truth.

Both grace and truth are Jesus personified. When you see what really is (truth), then Christ, who is in you, will set you free from trying to get back in God's good graces, trying to get *in*, because you will know the truth that you are *already in*!

You will then be able to experience and enjoy a new and better way of living ... new life in Christ. You will be:

- free from feeling like you have to perform to please God.
- free from fear, doubt, and anxiety.
- free from fear of being punished by an angry god.
- free from guilt, condemnation, and shame.
- free from fear of death.
- free from wondering which denomination or doctrine is 'right.'
- free from 'God's judgment.'
- free from judging others.
- free from excluding others.
- free to enjoy life.
- free to love.

In this new and better way of living, every day you find out that God is better than you thought the day before!

I hope you'll consider being convertible—having an open mind. Consider being open to seeing things differently than you have before. Consider being open to seeing things differently than religion teaches. God is in the revelation business; He is continually revealing to you how much better He is than you previously thought!

Of course, don't be gullible and fall for anything, but be willing to test what you hear and let God show you what really is.

CHAPTER 1
GOD IS LOVE

{Note}

I refer to the Trinity as follows:

The Father: 'Papa' (Jesus spoke Aramaic and used the term 'Abba' which was a term of loving endearment, much like a little child today would call their father 'Papa.')

Jesus: 'Jesus.'

The Holy Spirit: 'Sarayu,' which is a Native American term for 'wind.' Jesus said, "The wind blows wherever it pleases. You hear its sound, but you cannot tell where it comes from or where it is going. So it is with everyone born of the Spirit" (John 3:8). (From *The Shack* by William Paul Young.)

Be Willing to Change Your Mind About Love ...

Easter and Christmas are the two most important and most celebrated Christian days of the year. Most people know that Christmas celebrates Jesus's birth as a human being, and most people know that Easter celebrates Jesus's resurrection—when He rose from being crucified on the cross three days earlier.

Most churches and many Christians have a cross somewhere—prominently in the church building, on a necklace, or like my son, who has a big cross tattoo on his arm. However, I've found that not many of us know what the cross and Jesus's death and resurrection mean for us ... or for anyone else.

We have heard, and can repeat, that Jesus died for our sins and that He rose from the dead ... because, well ... just because?

For a long time, I believed and taught that Jesus rose from the dead to prove that He was God so that we would believe His teaching—sort of a validation deal. That's one theory.

I believe that Papa wants us to know the truth about Christmas, Easter, the cross and why those two and Sarayu started and continue everything They have done. It all starts with Their *unconditional love for YOU*!

"For God so *loved the world*, that He gave His only begotten Son, that whoever believes in Him shall not perish, but have eternal life" (John 3:16).

"And this is eternal life, that they may know You, the only true God, and Jesus Christ whom You have sent" (John 17:3).

"The Lord is not slow about His promise, as some count slowness, but is patient toward you, not wishing for any to perish but for all to come to repentance" (2 Peter 3:9).

Papa, Jesus, and Sarayu are all about helping us change our minds about Them and ourselves!

"The Greek word *metanoia*, poorly translated as 'repent' in the Bible (Matthew 3:2, Mark 1:15), quite literally means 'to change your mind.' Until the mind changes the very way it processes the moment, nothing changes long term" (Richard Rohr).

God Is Love

The most important foundational truth of all is to know that God *is* love. It is impossible for us to exaggerate or embellish God's love and His love for us. You won't see Jesus face to face and say, "Wow, I overestimated Your love and grace, Jesus … You're not nearly as good as I thought!"

1 John 4:8, 4:16—God is love.

God's very essence is love. Everything flows from His pure, agape love that always does what is best for the other person. Pastor Lee O'Hare's online post captures the essence of agape very well. He said, "The Greek word used here to describe and define God is the word 'AGAPE', which is a very precise and unique word used to describe a kind of love that is totally foreign to human experience. It could easily be translated 'the God kind of love.' It is not so much something that God HAS; it is rather who or what God IS. It is a love that is completely unconditional and that emanates from the very person and character of God which is always seeking the highest and the best and is not motivated in any degree by the loveliness or worthiness of its recipient."

Malcolm Smith said, "I may tell you that I have a glass of water or a reservoir of water, but it is an entirely different category to say that 'I am water!' To have water means my possession of it is subject to change whether by increase or decrease, but to BE water means I am never subject to change because that is what I am! God is the definition of love … that is what He is!"

Frederick Buechner said, "God does not need the Creation in order to have something to love … because within Himself love happens."

Love is also the ultimate prophetic purpose of God for us! For everyone's mutual benefit, God wants us to love each other as Jesus loves us—unconditionally and by giving up our rights, doing whatever is necessary to love!

John 13:34 (MIRROR): "I give you a new commandment, keep on loving one another just as I have loved you– my love for you is the source of your love for one another."

Some quotes on love by Steve McVey:

- "God loves you right where you are. No matter what you're doing or not doing."
- "God can't love you any more or any less than He does at this very moment."
- "The way we perceive God will guide the way we relate to others. God is love. Believe that and watch what happens in your relationships."
- "Divine love can be nothing less than perfect love."
- "God's love isn't predicated on our response. He loves because God is love."
- "Love always takes the initiative without waiting to see what its recipient will do first."
- "Divine love wants us to relax and simply enjoy our relationship to Him."

High Love

Ephesians 3:16–19 (Italics mine): I pray that out of His glorious riches He may strengthen you with power through His Spirit in your inner being, so that Christ may dwell in your hearts through faith. And I pray that you, being rooted and established in love, may have power, together with all the Lord's holy people, *to grasp how wide and long and high and deep is the love of Christ, and to know this love that surpasses knowledge*—that you may be filled to the measure of all the fullness of God.

'High' means above all; God's plan that supersedes everything else; God's ways are higher than ours.

We, all humans, tend to think, *God loves us and those in our group. But He can't possibly love other people. Look how bad they are. Look at the wrong beliefs they have. They don't believe in God.*

We think that, but the truth is, *God's love is at such a high level it's hard for us to comprehend it. It's unconditional and way better than any example of human love! It's the same for you … and everyone!*

Wide Love

Ephesians 3:17–19 (MIRROR) (Italics and parenthesis mine): "17 This will ignite your faith to fully grasp the reality of the indwelling Christ. *You are rooted and founded in love. Love is your invisible inner source,* just like the root system of a tree and the foundation of a building. (The dimensions of your inner person exceed any other capacity that could possibly define you.)

"18 Love is your reservoir of super human strength which causes you to see everyone equally sanctified in the context of the limitless extent of *love's breadth and length, and the extremities of its dimensions in depth and height.*

"19 I desire for you to become intimately acquainted with the *love of Christ* on the deepest possible level; far beyond the reach of a mere academic, intellectual grasp. Within the scope of this equation God finds the ultimate expression of himself in you. (So that you may be filled with all the fullness of God, awaken to the consciousness of His closeness! Separation is an illusion! Oneness was God's idea all along! He desires to express Himself through your touch, your voice, your presence; He is so happy to dwell in you! There is no place in the universe where He would rather be!)"

God's love is so wide; it encompasses everyone to the ends of the earth!

Long Love

Ephesians 3:16–19 (Italics mine): "I pray that out of His glorious riches He may strengthen you with power through His Spirit in your inner being, so that Christ may dwell in your hearts through faith. And I pray that you, being rooted and established in love, may have power, together with all the Lord's holy people, *to grasp how wide and long and high and deep is the love of Christ, and to know this love that surpasses knowledge*—that you may be filled to the measure of all the fullness of God."

Psalms 100:5 says, "For the Lord is good; His lovingkindness is everlasting and His faithfulness is to all generations."

Psalms 118 says five times that His lovingkindness is forever!

God's love is long love. It lasts forever, for all eternity. We can never be separated from God's love!

Contrary to what religion has incorrectly taught, there's no cutoff date at the end of this life. Death can't separate us from God's love!

Romans 8:35–39 says, "Who shall separate us from the love of Christ? Shall tribulation, or distress, or persecution, or famine, or nakedness, or peril, or sword…Yet in all these things we are more than conquerors through Him who loved us. For I am persuaded that neither death nor life, nor angels nor principalities nor powers, nor things present nor things to come, nor height nor depth, nor any other created thing, shall be able to separate us from the love of God which is in Christ Jesus our Lord."

Deep Love

Ephesians 3:16–19 (Italics mine): "I pray that out of His glorious riches He may strengthen you with power through His Spirit in your inner being, so that Christ may dwell in your hearts through faith. And I pray that you, being rooted and established in love, may have power, together with all the Lord's holy people, to *grasp how wide and long and high and deep is the love of Christ, and to know this love that surpasses knowledge*—that you may be filled to the measure of all the fullness of God."

When Jesus became our sin at the cross, He (and we with Him) died to sin. He went to the very depth of our sin with us and met us there. He took it all, experienced it all, took it all away and died to it all.

Saul of Tarsus was, in his own words, the worst sinner there was. Think of someone who hates Jesus, who hates Christians, who participated in the murder of Christians, who had authority and went around arresting Christians, taking them away from their family and livelihood and kept them in prison ... just for being Christians! Sounds like ISIS today.

God's love for Saul was so deep that He stopped him in his tracks and revealed that Jesus had always been in him ... since his birth!

Galatians 1:15–16 (MIRROR): "God's eternal love dream separated me from my mother's womb; His grace became my identity. This is the heart of the gospel that I proclaim; it began with an unveiling of sonship in me, freeing me to announce the same sonship in the masses of non-Jewish people." (Translator's note: "The Greek text is quite clear: 'It pleased the Father to reveal His Son in me in order that I may proclaim Him in the nations!' Not 'among' the Gentiles as most translations have it.")

The love of Christ can't be comprehended with human knowledge; it has to be revealed to us ... (that you may be filled with all the fullness of God). What enables us to realize, experience, enjoy and use all the fullness of God that we are already filled with is comprehending God's love!

Ask God to reveal His love to you today!

No Fear with This Love

When we grasp how God really loves us (which can't be understood humanly; it must be supernaturally revealed by God to our spirit and then believed by our mind), we need never be afraid of God for anything, including judgment! That's a new, and much better, way of living!

1 John 3:1 says, "Behold what manner of love the Father has bestowed on us, that we should be called children of God!"

Jesus calls us to love others with agape love, whether they are fellow believers (John 13:34) or bitter enemies (Matthew 5:44).

"This is how we know what love is: Jesus Christ laid down His life for us. And we ought to lay down our lives for our brothers and sisters" (1 John 3:16).

The opposite of unconditional love is when you think you are *not* loved unconditionally, and the result of that is fear.

1 John 4:16–19 says, "We have come to know and have believed the love which God has for us. God is love, and the one who abides in love abides in God, and God abides in him.

"By this, *love is perfected in us,* so that we may have *confidence in the day of judgment;* because as *He is, so also are we in this world.*

"There is *no fear in love;* but *perfect love casts out fear, because fear involves punishment,* and the *one who fears is not perfected in love. We love, because He first loved.*"

1 John 4:18 (AMP): "*There is no fear in love* [dread does not exist], but full-grown (complete, perfect) love turns fear out of doors *and* expels every trace of terror! For fear brings with it the thought of punishment, and [so] he who is afraid has not reached the full maturity of love [is not yet grown into love's complete perfection]."

The Only Thing That Counts

In 1 Corinthians 13, 'love' in the original text is 'agape,' which is only used in the New Testament (and other writings) as God's supernatural love. God is love, and so it's consistent with scripture to say 'God' or 'Jesus' instead of 'love' in this chapter. When considering anything about God, we start with the filter that *He is love and everything else He is and does flows from His unconditional agape love.*

1 Corinthians 13 (Parenthesis and italics mine): "Love (God) is patient and does not give up; Love (God) is kind; Love (God) is not jealous and does not envy and thinks no evil; Love (God) does not brag or boast *and* is not arrogant or proud; Love (God) does not act unbecomingly or dishonor others; Love (God) does not seek its own … is not self-seeking. Love (God) does not insist on its own rights *or* its own way; Love (God) is not provoked and is not irritable and puts up with anything. Love (God) does not take into account a wrong *suffered– keeps no record of wrong;* Love (God) does not rejoice in unrighteousness and is not happy with sin. Love (God) rejoices with the truth; Love (God) bears all things and always protects. Love (God) believes all things, always trusts, and is ever ready to believe the best of every person. Love (God) hopes all things; Love (God) endures all things and always perseveres. Love (God) never fails and never comes to an end."

Galatians 5:6 (Parenthesis and italics mine): "The only thing that counts (what is important) is *faith expressed as love.*"

Perfect Love

God is love, love of a different kind than we usually experience. God's love is perfect, unconditional love.

When a person first starts to learn that God's love is unconditional, their response is almost always, "Yes, but what about …?" And it probably takes a lifetime for us to really grasp and believe that there are absolutely no conditions to God's perfect love.

Believing that God's love has no conditions requires a drastic change of mind! The Greek word *metanoia* that translators incorrectly translate 'repent' literally means 'a radical mind shift.'

We have been indoctrinated by religious teaching (based on a lie from early translators who raised money for building huge cathedrals and for leadership wealth) that repent means something like "remorsefully and sincerely groveling before a harsh, punitive god who will retributively withdraw its love and favor and ultimately torture you forever if you don't." That's far different from a radical mind shift.

So, ironically, it actually takes a radical mind shift to leave that perverted teaching and turn to believing the truth that God's love is perfect! God loves the imperfect (us) perfectly—which means unconditionally, without any conditions, limits or provisions.

Many 'Christians' will give pseudo assent that God's love is unconditional and then add "but …" and they insert the first of many conditions!

Our loving Papa wants us to develop the radical mindset of taking Him at His word and believing that His love for us … and everyone … is indeed unconditional!

As we come to believe that more and more, life gets better and better and better! So, we constantly remind ourselves that God's love has no conditions.

God Got Rid of His Record Collection

1 Corinthians 13:5 (Parenthesis mine): "Love (God) keeps no record of wrongs."

Santa Claus is not real, and neither is the fictitious god who's 'making a list and checking it twice.' Taking the following verses to the Holy Spirit and asking Him to reveal to you what they truly mean will start building a foundation for you that will enable you to *see what really is* and experience a new and better way of life!

Knowing and remembering that God absolutely keeps no record of your wrongs will enable you to relate to Him as the loving Father He really is.

Knowing and remembering that God absolutely keeps no record of your wrongs frees you from all fear of judgment and punishment!

John 1:29 (Parenthesis mine): "Behold, the Lamb of God (Jesus) who comes to take away the sin of the world."

2 Corinthians 5:19 says, "Christ is proof that God reconciled the total cosmos to Himself. Deity and humanity embraced in Christ; the fallen state of mankind was deleted; their trespasses would no longer count against them! God has placed this message within us. He now announces His friendship with every individual from within us! (God [The Father] was in Christ reconciling the world [cosmos] to Himself, not counting [or imputing] their trespasses [or sins] against them.)"

In Colossians 1:13–14, 2:13, the Bible says, "He rescued us from the dominion of darkness and relocated us into the kingdom where the love of His Son rules. In God's mind, mankind is associated in Christ; in His blood sacrifice, we were ransomed; our redemption was secured; our sins were completely done away with. You were once spiritually dead, as confirmed in your constant failure; being bound to a lifestyle ruled by the distorted desires of the flesh, but now God has made you alive together with Him, having forgiven you all your trespasses and sins."

Isaiah 43:25 (Italics mine): "I The Lord, *even* I, *am* He who blots out your transgressions for My own sake; and I will not remember your sins."

Hebrews 8:11–12 says, "Knowing Me will no longer be a Sunday-school lesson, or something taught by persuasive words of doctrine, neither will they *know* Me on account of family tradition or door to door evangelism. Everyone, from the most unlikely to the most prominent people in society, will know Me inwardly. This knowledge of Me will never again be based on a sin-consciousness. My act of mercy, extended in Christ as the new Covenant, has removed every possible definition of sin from memory."

CHAPTER 2
GOD IS LOVE IN COMMUNITY

"The grace of the Lord Jesus Christ, and the love of God, and the fellowship of the Holy Spirit, be with you all" (2 Corinthians 13:14).

BFFs

"What would it be like for you to have three faithful friends who loved you unconditionally, thought about you all the time, delighted in being with you and were continually filled with joy about being best friends forever with you? We don't want you to wonder! We want you to *know*! That's how We feel about YOU ... today, all day, and every day!" ~Love, Jesus, Papa, and Sarayu.

Before there was anything that we know about in creation, God existed ... in community. God has always been three distinct entities—God the Father, Jesus the Son, and the Holy Spirit.

Christians call that the Trinity—the Three in One. While we can't fully comprehend One God, with one essence being three entities, it's essential for us to embrace that concept in order to understand God's nature, and thus know who God is, who we are and why we're here.

The essential thing we need to know is that God has always existed in community. God has never been a single solitary entity existing by Himself. Community (being together in relationship) is who God is. Relationship is foundationally what God is all about.

God wants to have a relationship with you. That's what They think about all the time. That's what drives Them. When you start to know and are continually aware of and believe that God, above all, wants to have a relationship with you, that will change everything! That's *seeing what really is:* a new and better way of life!

Loving Relationships

You can sum up what Jesus, Papa, and Sarayu are all about in two words: *loving relationships!*

Loving relationships are what the Trinity is all about, what They have always prioritized, and what They desire for all of us ... with Them. *And They will not be denied!*

They created Paradise, then created the first man and woman, and the very first act that ever happened was ... what? What do you think?

Genesis 1:27 (Italics mine): "So God created man in His *own* image; in the image of God He created him; male and female He created them. Then God blessed them ..."

'God' comes from the Hebrew word Elohiym, which means divine ones, Gods. It's plural, meaning the Trinity. 'Blessed' in the original Hebrew meant to bless, kneel, adore, worship, praise, salute.

The very first thing Adam saw was the Trinity—Jesus, Papa, and the Holy Spirit kneeling, praising, adoring and worshipping him, their new friend ... as he represented all humans who would come after him.

Let that soak in a minute. Think about Jesus, Papa, and the Holy Spirit kneeling at this creation They had so meticulously planned and finally created and worshipping him ... Can you get a sense of how They felt about him? *Can you see Their love?*

When we worship God, that's our love responding to Their love!

Someone to Love

When the Apostle Paul wrote the first chapter of Ephesians, verses 3 through 14 are basically one elongated thought (there were no sentences, periods or verses in the original Greek) summing up what God did for us before creation because of the love They have always had for us.

Any of you who are parents know a little bit about what I'm talking about. Once you learned that you were going to have a baby (expand your community), you started making plans. You may have remodeled a room. You bought new furniture. You started getting blankets and onesies. You knew in advance you would love your new addition. You can remember seeing your newborn baby for the first time, and it was instant love. *Love!*

Parents, when you saw your baby for the first time, did you focus on right and wrong/morality? Is that what you were all consumed with? Or were you consumed with love?

God could have focused on right and wrong/morality. After all, being omniscient, God knew what was going to happen. However, because of Their great love, They took care of everything in advance. In the following great passage, the phrase 'in love' or 'because of their great love' refers to Their mindset and motivation for everything They did for us before creation!

Ephesians 1:2–10 (Italics mine): "Grace to you and peace from God our Father and the Lord Jesus Christ. Blessed *be* the God and Father of our Lord Jesus Christ, who has blessed us with every spiritual blessing in the heavenly *places* in Christ, just as *He chose us in Him before the foundation of the world*, that we should be holy and without blame before Him *in love, having* predestined us to adoption as sons by Jesus Christ to Himself, according to the good pleasure of His will, to the praise of the glory of His grace, by which He made us accepted in the Beloved.

"In Him we have redemption through His blood, the forgiveness of sins, according to the riches of His grace which He made to abound toward us in all wisdom and prudence, having made known to us the mystery of His will, according to His good pleasure which He purposed in Himself, that in the dispensation of the fullness of the times He might gather together in one all things in Christ, both which are in heaven and which are on earth– in Him."

God is all about community: Including us in Their divine triune circle dance of grace: God's unconditional love in perpetual action working all things for the good of everyone, bringing about the restoration of all!

First Love

Can you remember your first love? God has always been love … in community.

C.S. Lewis said, "All sorts of people are fond of repeating the Christian statement that 'God is love.' But they seem not to notice that the words 'God is love' have no real meaning unless God contains at least two Persons. Love is something one person has for another person. If God was a single person, then before the world was made, He was not love."

Notice how Baxter Kruger paraphrases John 1:1–2, "Before the time of the beginning the Word (Jesus) was face to face with God. He was there before the ages in *intimate union* with God, and fully God."

God's community of love is really hard for us to fathom because, humanly speaking, we have nothing to compare it with. God transformed the early church from a people who believed in a single, solitary, angry god who was not relational and was not experienced in community, into a people who experienced authentic community with Jesus, Papa, and the Holy Spirit. They coined a word for this new experience of community—perichoresis.

"Genuine acceptance removes fear and hiding, and creates freedom to know and be known. In this freedom arises a fellowship and sharing so honest, open and real that the persons involved dwell in one another. There is union without loss of individual identity. When one weeps, the other tastes salt. It is only in the Triune relationship of Father, Son and Spirit that personal relationship of this order exists, and the early Church used the word 'perichoresis' to describe it. The good news is that Jesus Christ has drawn us within this relationship and its fullness and life are to be played out in each of us and in all creation" (C. Baxter Kruger, *God Is For Us.*)

Love In Community

While many Christians are aware of the term 'Trinity,' few of us know what it means, and sadly, fewer still have any concept of its importance.

C.S. Lewis and others have referred to the relationship of Father, Son, and Spirit as a dance. In borrowing from Lewis, Dr. Steve McVey, Dr. Baxter Kruger, and other Trinitarian writers, I view Their relationship (in which They have already included us!) as Their Divine Triune circle dance of unconditional love and everything that flows from Their love: joy, peace, patience, kindness, goodness, gentleness, faith, compassion, mercy, grace, and so much more!

In his article titled *The Trinitarian Vision,* Baxter Kruger states, "From all eternity, God is not alone and solitary, but lives as Father, Son and Spirit in a rich and glorious and abounding fellowship of utter oneness. There is no darkness or emptiness in this circle, no depression or fear or insecurity. The Trinitarian life is a great dance of unchained communion and intimacy, fired by passionate, self-giving and other-centered love and mutual delight. This life is good. It is right, unique, full of music and joy, blessedness and peace. Such love, giving rise to such togetherness and fellowship and oneness, is the womb of the universe and of humanity within it." This is truly a new and better way of life!

Fleshing out Community – Part I

God is love, and God is love in community. What does that have to do with me? Why should I care?

It has everything to do with why God created us, to begin with, and what His (Their) plan has always been! Understanding this is the beginning of grasping *the meaning of life!*

More from *The Trinitarian Vision* by Baxter Kruger: "The stunning truth is that this Triune God, in amazing and lavish love, determined to open the circle and share the Trinitarian life with others. This is the one, eternal and abiding reason for the creation of the world and of human life. There is no other God, no other will of God, no second plan, no hidden agenda for human beings. Before the creation of the world, the Father, Son and Spirit set their love upon us and planned to bring us to share and know and experience the Trinitarian life itself. Unto this end the cosmos was called into being, and the human race was fashioned, and Adam and Eve were given a place in the coming of Jesus Christ, the Father's Son himself, in and through whom the dream of our adoption would be accomplished."

They have in mind for us a new and much better way of life!

Fleshing out Community – Part II

In the Mirror Bible paraphrase, Francois Du Toit has a wonderful way of helping us *see what really is.* The Mirror is a divinely insightful, life-giving and transformational translation. In the words of Francois' fellow South African and former secretary general of the Evangelical Fellowship of Zimbabwe, Rev. Anouya Andrew Muchechetere, the Mirror is, "A welcome revelatory and revolutionary development that is divinely sanctioned, inspired and directed. This translation is by no doubt a compelling grounding expository of our century. To God be the Glory."

Following is the mirror paraphrase of Ephesians 1:8–11: "This grace shown towards us communicates a wisdom and discernment of our worth that completely surpasses any definition. The secret is out! His cherished love dream now unfolds in front of our very eyes. In the economy of the fullness of time, everything culminates in Christ; all that is in heaven and all that is on earth is reconciled in Him. This is how we fit into God's picture: Christ is the measure of our portion, we are in Him, invented and defined in Him. God's blueprint intention is on exhibition in us. Everything He accomplishes is inspired by the energy and intent of His affection."

More from *The Trinitarian Vision* by Baxter Kruger: "Before creation, it was decided that the Son would cross every chasm between the Triune God and humanity and establish a real and abiding relationship with us– union. Jesus was predestined to be the mediator, the one in and through whom the very life of the Triune God would enter human existence, and human existence would be lifted up to share in the Trinitarian life."

Fleshing out Community – Part III

They did it together! The very essence of the Trinity, Their oneness, has always been, is now and always will be. They have always been one, have never been separated, and never will be.

One of the greatest, most tragic, most damaging lies that religion has foisted off on us is the *lie of separation.* This lie rips the very fabric of God and damages the human soul in almost irreparable ways. Thank God it's *almost.*

One of Jesus's core teachings is the contrast between darkness and light. I believe that the *lie of separation* IS the *great* darkness. We have been taught the horrendous lie that we have caused God to separate Himself from us because of our 'inherited sin' and that the ultimate result of our actions was God the Father separating Himself from Jesus at the cross and 'pouring out all His wrath' on Jesus. We've heard that so often by so many people that many 'Christians' have never questioned it. On the other hand, the watching world has seen the incompatible dichotomy of saying, "God is love, and God is one …" and in the next breath saying, "God is not loving at all and is separate …" as being, well … unbelievable. So, the multitudes have walked away from organized religion.

Fortunately, the truth will set us free from those lies!

More from *The Trinitarian Vision* by Baxter Kruger: "When Adam and Eve rebelled, ushering in chaos and misery into God's creation, the Father, Son and Spirit never abandoned Their dream, but wonderfully incorporated darkness and sin into the tapestry of the coming incarnation. As the Father's Son became human, and as He submitted Himself to bear our anger, and bizarre blindness, and as He gave himself to suffer a murderous death at our hands, He established a real and abiding relationship with fallen humanity at our very worst– and He brought His Father and the Holy Spirit with Him. It was in Jesus himself, and in His death at our bitter hands, that the Trinitarian life of God pitched its tent in our hell on earth, thereby uniting all that the Father, Son and Spirit share with all that we are in our brokenness, shame and sin– adoption."

Fleshing Out Community –
Part IV: How Did They Do It?

I grew up in a Christian home and had wonderful, loving parents who loved God and were very involved in their church. I was in the church pretty much every time the doors were opened. Although I continued my church attendance after I left home, it was in large part because of 'duty' and, in reality, more cosmetic than spiritual.

I knew that Jesus went to the cross for my sins and that He saved me. That was about all I knew. I never thought much more about it.

However, as I started to learn what really happened and why, I finally started to see what really is, and started to enjoy a new, and much better, way of life.

Baxter Kruger gives us great insight in his final words in *The Trinitarian Vision*. "In the life and death of Jesus, the Holy Spirit made His way into human pain and blindness. Inside our broken inner worlds, the Spirit works to reveal Jesus *in* us so that we can meet Jesus Himself in our own sin and shame, and begin to see what Jesus sees, and know His Father with Him. The Holy Spirit *takes of* Jesus and discloses it to us, so that we can know and experience Jesus' own relationship with His Father, and we can be free to live in the Father's embrace with Jesus. As the Spirit works we are summoned to take sides with Jesus against our own darkness and prejudice, and take simple steps of trust and change. As we do, Jesus' own anointing with the Spirit– His own fellowship with His Father, His own unearthly assurance, His own freedom and joy and power in the Spirit– begin to form in us, while not diminishing but augmenting and freeing our own uniqueness as persons. The Spirit's passion is to bring His anointing of Jesus to full and personal and abiding expression in us as unique persons, and not only in us personally, but in our relationship with the Father in Jesus, and in our relationships with one another, and indeed with all creation, until the whole cosmos is a living sacrament of the great dance of the Triune God."

Loving and Living in Community

We're learning that God is love and God is community (Father, Son, and Spirit), and They have included us in Their community! And They have included everyone else!

But ... we're all different! We believe different things; we have different values. We live differently. We're all selfish and self-centered to some degree, especially with *that boss of ours* and *that neighbor who has the loud angry dogs and hosts the loud, late-night parties and that person who gossips* and *lies about me.* How do I live in community with them? Do I have to? Yeah, I sometimes feel that way too.

Humanly speaking, it's impossible. But with God, all things are possible! Trying, by our own resources, to be loving to hard-to-love people is a set-up for failure. Only Jesus can love like only Jesus loves. However, the really good news is that Jesus lives in us and He wants to live as us and through us! As we rest in Him, trust Him and allow Him; we participate with Him living through our personalities and speech.

1 Corinthians 13 (Parenthesis mine): "Love (God) is patient and does not give up; Love (God) is kind; Love (God) is not jealous and does not envy and thinks no evil; Love (God) does not brag or boast and is not arrogant or proud; Love (God) does not act unbecomingly or dishonor others; Love (God) does not seek its own ... is not self-seeking. Love (God) does not insist on its own rights or its own way; Love (God) is not provoked and is not irritable and puts up with anything. Love (God) does not take into account a wrong suffered– keeps no record of wrong; Love (God) does not rejoice in unrighteousness and is not happy with sin. Love (God) rejoices with the truth; Love (God) bears all things and always protects. Love (God) believes all things, always trusts, and is ever ready to believe the best of every person. Love (God) hopes all things; Love (God) endures all things and always perseveres. Love (God) never fails and never comes to an end."

Letting Christ live and love as us and through us brings a new, and much better, way of life!

CHAPTER 3
JESUS IS GRACE

Grace Is

Grace is God's unconditional love and pure goodness perpetually in action working all things for the good (Divine Influence) to help everyone know and enjoy and experience abundant life by:

- Relating to us personally.
- Energizing and empowering us to be all God created us to be.
- Energizing and empowering us to do all God created us to do.
- Continually showing us that God is PURE goodness.
- Continually showing us that God is totally for us.
- Continually showing us that God has forgiven, accepted and included us in Their relationship and chose us before creation.
- Continually reminding us that there is not and never has been separation from God for anyone.
- Communicating with us how They see us and everyone.
- Continually reminding us that we died, we no longer live but Christ lives in us, through us and as us.
- Reminding us that we are one with the Father, Jesus, the Holy Spirit … and everyone.
- Reminding us that They are working every situation for the good of us and everyone.
- Producing effortless change in us as we dwell in seamless union with the Trinity.
- Grace is a Person, continually revealing to us what God wants us to say and do in every situation

Grace is God's unconditional love and pure goodness perpetually in action flowing:

- From the Trinity to us.
- From us to ourselves.
- From us to others.
- Producing from others to us.

This perpetual motion of grace is the kingdom of God/kingdom of heaven!

2 Corinthians 13:14 says, "The grace of the Lord Jesus Christ, and the love of God, and the fellowship of the Holy Spirit, be with you all."

Because we have an enemy who does not want us to know and remember this, and because we tend to forget, we want to continually remind ourselves and each other of these truths.

doesn't / love

Jesus Is Grace

Definitions of grace abound, so that you'll know how to interpret my intent in this book, my working definition is: Grace is God's free, unrequested, unmerited gift which was given in Christ to all people prior to creation and was manifested in time and space at Jesus's finished work at the cross. God's grace is the Father, Jesus, and the Holy Spirit's unilateral (one-way, with nothing expected or demanded in return) expression of:

- unconditional agape love.
- unconditional forgiveness of all sin.
- total acceptance.
- universal inclusion of all.

Grace includes, but is not limited to God:

- eliminating everything that we falsely believed caused us to be separated from Him.
- creating everyone as new creations who are pure, holy, innocent, without fault and *right* with God forever.
- indwelling us all forever with the Holy Spirit of Christ providing us Holy Spirit power.
- effortlessly living Christ's life in us, as us and through us.

Grace is totally a free gift from God and requires no request or any action on our part!

When a person hears the good news of the Grace of Jesus Christ, the Holy Spirit gives them the Faith of Christ to believe what is already true. Then a person *grows in grace* as the Holy Spirit continues to reveal the things that have been freely given to us by God.

1 Corinthians 2:12 says, "Now we have received, not the spirit of the world, but the Spirit who is from God, that we might know the things that have been freely given to us by God."

Resist "But What About …?"

Now that we have a working definition of grace, I encourage you to suspend whatever you may have been taught about grace in the past … at least until the end of this chapter. Ask the Holy Spirit of Christ to reveal the Truth of Christ to you. For now, be willing to resist the temptation to jump to "But what about (the verse of choice that 'seems' to contradict pure grace)?"

Growing in grace requires letting the Teacher be the Teacher and our being the one who is being taught.

Hebrews 8:10–13 (MIRROR): "Now, instead of documenting my laws on stone, I will chisel them into your mind and engrave them in your inner consciousness; it will no longer be a one-sided affair. I will be your God and you will be my people, not by compulsion, but by mutual desire. Knowing me will no longer be a Sunday-school lesson, or something taught by persuasive words of doctrine, neither will they know me on account of family tradition or door to door evangelism. Everyone, from the most unlikely to the most prominent people in society, will know me inwardly. This knowledge of me will never again be based on a sin-consciousness. My act of mercy, extended in Christ as the new Covenant, has removed every possible definition of sin from memory!"

He announces the new dispensation to confirm that the old shadow system has been redundant. (When He said, "A new covenant," He has made the first (the law) obsolete. But whatever is becoming obsolete and growing old is ready to disappear.)

John 16:13–15 (NLT): "When the Spirit of truth comes, He will guide you into all truth. He will not speak on his own but will tell you what he has heard. He will tell you about the future. He will bring Me glory by telling you whatever he receives from Me. All that belongs to the Father is Mine; this is why I said, 'The Spirit will tell you whatever He receives from me.'"

Religion's False 'Means of Grace'

Religion has taught a variety of half-truths and untruths about the 'means of grace,' meaning "things we can do to get God to give us grace." That whole concept flies in the face of the very meaning of grace!

By its very definition, Grace is a free, unrequested, unmerited gift! God's will and purpose since before creation was to give us grace.

2 Timothy 1:9–10 (Italics mine): "God has saved us and called us with a holy calling, not according to our works, but according to *His own purpose and grace which was given to us in Christ Jesus before time began,* but has now *been revealed by the appearing of our Savior Jesus Christ,* who has abolished death and brought life and immortality to light through the gospel."

Religion considers grace to be a 'doctrine,' but doctrines don't 'appear' and doctrines don't 'teach.' Christ in us teaches us!

Titus 2:11–12 (Italics mine): "The *grace of God has appeared, bringing salvation to all men, instructing us* to deny ungodliness and worldly desires and to live sensibly, righteously and godly in the present age."

John writes that they saw Jesus's glory—*full of grace and truth.* Jesus is grace! John 1:14–18 (Parenthesis and italics mine): "And the Word (Jesus) became flesh, and dwelt among us, and we saw His glory, glory as of the only begotten from the Father, full of grace and truth. For of His fullness we have all received, *grace upon grace.* For the Law was given through Moses; grace and truth were realized through Jesus Christ. No one has seen God at any time; the only begotten God who is in the bosom of the Father, He has explained *Him.*"

Ephesians 2:8–9 (MIRROR): "Your salvation is not a reward for good behavior! It was a grace thing from start to finish; you had no hand in it. Even the gift to believe simply reflects His (Christ's) faith! By grace you are! Saved by the gift of faith; grace reveals who we are, and the faith of God persuades us of it! You did not invent faith; it was God's faith to begin with! It is from faith to faith, (Romans 1:17)."

Grace is Many-Faceted

The Holy Spirit in us reveals to us the many facets of grace …
although eternity isn't long enough to ever see them all!

1 Corinthians 2:12 (MIRROR): "The Spirit proceeding from
God unveils the gifts of His generosity. He has graced us with
understanding so that we may know what He has always had in
mind for us; this is so unlike the secular spirit of the wisdom of
the world where everything has a price tag!"

Christ is the unveiling of the mystery of God's wisdom: now
we know how God redeemed our righteousness and our wholeness in Christ. In God's economy, Christ represents us; what man
could never achieve through personal discipline and willpower
as taught in every religion, God's faith accomplished in Christ.
Of His design are we in Christ; we are associated in oneness with
Him. Our wisdom is sourced in this union! Also, our righteousness and holiness originate from Him.

Holiness equals wholeness and harmony of man's spirit, soul,
and body. Our redemption is sanctioned in Him. He redeemed
our identity, our sanity, our health, our joy, our peace, our innocence and our complete well-being! Secular religion is the prod-
uct of the spirit of this world where everything is performance
based; only the heroes of the moment are acclaimed; the rest are
reduced to spectators and audience.

Ephesians 2:4–7 says, "God, who is rich in mercy, because
of His great love with which He loved us, even when we were
dead in trespasses, made us alive together with Christ (by grace
you have been saved), and raised us up together, and made us sit
together in the heavenly places in Christ Jesus, that in the ages
to come He might show the exceeding riches of His grace in His
kindness toward us."

The Ability to Respond

Many Christ-followers are familiar with the following verse: "Grow in the grace and knowledge of our Lord and Savior Jesus Christ. To Him be the glory both now and forever. Amen" (2 Peter 3:18).

Peter is encouraging us to grow in the knowledge *of* God—not what we think we know about God, but in God's own knowledge that He gives to us—the mind of Christ! The way to *grow in the knowledge* is to *grow in grace!*

Growing in grace is not something that we work at to bring about by our own effort. Growing in grace is "growing in the experience of Grace … Jesus Himself … living in us, as us and through us!"

Most people who have been involved in a church or parachurch ministry have been encouraged to grow spiritually, to become spiritually mature. Unfortunately, most of us have been taught that it is our responsibility and duty to do this by our own effort, which is totally contrary to the Grace of our Lord Jesus Christ!

'Responsibility' literally means 'the ability to respond.' Our growth only comes as we respond to Christ in us, who reveals His truth and causes us to grow!

No plant, fruit, or tree can cause itself to grow! Humans can facilitate some areas of our growth (bodybuilders), but we have no control over how tall we'll be, what our bone density will be, etc.

It's God who causes our growth. He has given us the ability to respond to His initiative.

1 Corinthians 3:6 (Paul): 'I planted, Apollos watered, but God was causing the growth."

(MIRROR): "I have planted, by bringing the gospel to you in the first place, then Apollos watered the seed in his ministry to you; but God causes the Christ life to ignite and expand in you."

The Gift of Grace

Do you give much thought to the gifts you give? Some People just want money. Some prefer gift cards.

These days my wife and I don't need a lot, so we prefer to give each other gifts that we know we're going to use anyway. For example, we recently gave birthday gifts of tickets to a Royals baseball game for me and Home Depot gift cards for her.

Did you know that the Greek word for birthday gift is 'charis'—which we translate as joy ... or grace?

2,000 years ago, a lot of thought went into giving gifts. There was no internet, there were no shopping malls, no gift catalogs, no gift cards. Then, the concept was that what the gift was worth indicated the value or worth that the giver placed on the person receiving the gift.

Thought went into giving a gift ... i.e. it would need to be something the receiving person would really like, that would also be useful and beneficial. Its worth would convey to the recipient what the giver thinks about them, how much they value them.

The ultimate gift would be something so astounding that the recipient would exclaim, "Wow! You think that much of me? That's too good to be true!"

Actually, the New Testament word that we translate as 'grace' means something way more than just 'birthday gift'—it's so utterly astounding that we think it must be too good to be true.

We throw the word grace around a lot. We say grace before meals. We sing *Amazing Grace*. We have doctrines of grace, but we're really in the dark when it comes to what grace actually means in its original use.

The primary reason that we don't know the true meaning of grace is that the whole objective of evil is to keep us from knowing Grace!

In 2 Corinthians 10:3–5, Paul shows us that what the enemy is ultimately doing is coming against our knowledge of God, specifically, our knowing that Jesus *is* Grace personified!

Evil's Goal

Evil's goal is to keep us from knowing God—from our personally and intimately knowing God—who God is and what God is like in every moment of our life! Knowing what Jesus is thinking and what He wants at any given moment.

The evil one knows that when we actually know the only true God, when we know He *is* Grace, then evil has lost all influence on us. So, he tries to keep us in the dark.

Suspend reality for a moment and picture a man and a woman. Imagine, if you will, the man saying, "I think so much of you that I want to demonstrate my love to you in the greatest way possible. I choose you to be my bride. I love you unconditionally, and I always will. I want to give you the mother of all gifts! It's this: I forgive you in advance for everything you might ever do to me. You are mine, and we are one forever. Everything I have is yours. You can't make me love you any more or any less. I have no demands of you. I will help you fulfill your potential to the max. I want you to enjoy me and my family forever.

"We are all full of joy, peace, patience, and we're totally good. There is nothing bad in any of us. We're always gentle and kind, and we're totally faithful, even if you aren't. When you mess up, we never, ever condemn you. We don't give you what you think you deserve. We call that mercy. Even when you do mess up, we give you what you think you don't deserve ... our unconditional love, forgiveness, and acceptance. We call that grace. I love you and am always for you, and I so hate anything that hurts you that I will ultimately get rid of it all and ultimately make all things right. I call that justice."

Can you imagine a husband like that? Would anyone ever be able to deserve a husband like that? Could you ever *repay* a husband like that? Could you ever *earn* a husband like that?

What if you thought, *This is SO good ... I'm just going to do whatever I want ... see if I can really get away with it. I'll stay out late, have affairs with others, mock and make fun of my husband, do whatever I want just to see if he really keeps his promise.* Some of us might be tempted to do that. Would you?

"That's Not Fair!"

What if you rebelled and betrayed a husband like we imagined yesterday? Of course, things wouldn't turn out well. Imagine that you eventually went back to that husband, and he kept his promise! He did what he said … kept his word … still loved you unconditionally and accepted you completely.

I would think that eventually there would come a time when you fully believed, relaxed, rested and started spending all your time with a spouse like that … because they're so good.

You'd also want to tell all your friends, right? "Hey, guys! You can't imagine how good my husband is … let me tell you!"

Now, suppose someone else came along and saw and heard about you and your spouse, and they said, "Your husband's not that good at all. He's not like you think. He's very demanding. He gets angry with everyone. He has limits to his love; in fact, he hates a lot of people, to begin with, and doesn't even give them a chance. It's impossible to please him."

How would you feel about the person making those complaints?

Pretend that happens, and you go to your husband, who is all good, and you tell him what that other person says. He tells you, "I know what they say, but it's not true. They have been deceived. They are in the dark. They have believed lies from someone who's against me. They are not my enemies; they just think they are. I and my family love that person … just like we love you."

How would you feel? You might think, *That's not fair! They don't deserve it. They should be punished! You can't be that good! You can't be so good that you love them too!*

Of course, anyone who says that is forgetting that they didn't do anything to deserve this husband's love, to begin with, either!

Now you know that I'm simply taking what scripture says about Jesus, His Father (the only true God), and the Holy Spirit, and putting those truths into that little imaginary husband and wife thing. Except, it's not imaginary. It's real!

Powerfully Unstoppable

Once we know the truth (the Good News), we are set free from bondage to the flesh, to sin and to evil.

Once we know the truth, the Good News, we are unstoppable! Once we know the truth and live like we know the truth, people see Jesus and are attracted to Him.

But if you don't know the truth, you will live in the dark. You will believe lies about God, yourself and evil. You will think you *are* evil because you 'do bad things.' You will think you have to fear God and work to please Him, and you know it's impossible to do.

You'll think sometimes you're good with Him, sometimes you're not. You'll judge and exclude others. You'll think you and your group are in with God because you do the right things ... and everyone else is out, excluded. You won't have any confidence or assurance. You won't really know God. You won't experience the abundant life Jesus came for you to enjoy ...

You won't have power ... you will be ripped off. You will be settling for way less, and you'll think that's as good as it gets. You will live a life cheated of the best. You won't even be close to the best, which is not only yours to have and enjoy—it's what God wants you to enjoy.

You will spend your life on a hamster wheel ... trying and trying and trying to get something that's elusive—and deep down, you know you'll never get it.

Your life will not be nearly as good as it can be because you've been ripped off!

Sometime people eventually quit trying, give up and try to get happiness in all the wrong places. (By the way, religion is one of those wrong places.)

God wants your marriages to be as good as possible. He wants your family relationships and your friendships to be as good as possible. He doesn't want you to continue to be ripped off.

Many people are being ripped off and don't even know it. To get out of the darkness, see the light and live by the light and thus not get ripped off, the first step is to see the light of God's love.

'Ripped Off' No More

Regarding seeing the light of God's love to help us keep from being ripped off, the apostle Paul wrote:

"If I speak in the tongues of men or of angels, but do not have love, I am only a resounding gong or a clanging cymbal. If I have the gift of prophecy and can fathom all mysteries and all knowledge, and if I have a faith that can move mountains, but do not have love, I am nothing. If I give all I possess to the poor and give over my body to hardship that I may boast, but do not have love, I gain nothing" (1 Corinthians 13:1–3).

See, no matter how good our techniques are, how smart we are, or how much we understand psychology ... no matter how many classes we take, how many Bible verses we memorize, or how many times we read and memorize Psalms and Proverbs ... if we don't love unconditionally, with no limits, and always do what is best for the other person ... it gains us nothing. Religion and the flesh will confirm that—but they will lie and say that you must now, by your own effort, change your selfish ways and start to love people like God loves you.

That's a very damaging lie ... because it's impossible! There is another way, and only one way to love like God loves us, and it has to do with the true definition of Grace.

We learned that the original meaning of the Greek word *charis*—which we translate in the Bible as *grace*—is a *birthday gift*. We learned that 2,000 years ago, a lot of thought went into giving gifts. The concept was that what the gift was worth indicated the value or worth that the giver placed on the person receiving the gift.

Let's start to tie things together and see exactly what the free gift of grace that we received as a result of Jesus's finished work at the cross is. When you understand this, you'll no longer get ripped off!

John 1:1–8 tells us Jesus was the Light of men. The Light shines in the darkness, and the darkness did not comprehend it. Jesus is God! He is The Word of God! He is The Light! Those aren't just descriptions ... that's who and what Jesus is!

Jesus (God) is Full of Grace and Truth

John 1:9–18 (Parenthesis and italics mine): "There was the true Light which, coming into the world, enlightens every man. He was in the world, and the world was made through (Jesus) and the world did not know (Jesus). Jesus came to His own, and those who were His own did not receive Jesus. But as many as received Jesus, to them He gave the right to become children of God, *even* to those who believe in His name, who were born, not of blood nor of the will of the flesh nor of the will of man, but of God. And the Word (Jesus) became flesh, and dwelt among us, and we saw His glory, glory as of the only begotten from the Father, *full* of grace and truth. For of His fullness we have all received, *grace upon grace.* For the Law was given through Moses; *grace and truth were realized through Jesus Christ.* No one has seen God at any time; the only begotten God who is in the bosom of the Father, but Jesus has revealed *Him.*"

I want you to see that Jesus is God; Jesus is full of Grace and truth; through His Holy Spirit, He is enlightening every one of us right now; we have *grace upon grace.*

In addition to being God, the Word of God, *Jesus is Grace!*

Titus 2:11–12 (Italics mine): "The *grace of God has appeared, bringing salvation to all men, instructing us* to deny ungodliness and worldly desires and to live sensibly, righteously and godly in the present age."

Look at this closely: the grace of God APPEARED! What or who appeared? A doctrine? A nice thought? A prayer that we say when we eat? God's Riches At Christ's Expense? (The inadequate and inaccurate religious acronym for grace.)

If you believe the lie that grace is anything other than *Jesus Himself,* you're being ripped off!

Jesus appeared! Jesus brought salvation to *all* people! The Holy Spirit of Jesus, in us, instructs us!

Jesus is not only full of Grace … Jesus is grace.

Don't ever be influenced by evil to gloss over grace, diminish grace, or think that there must be more to our relationship with God than *just grace. Never*! Jesus is *GRACE*!

Grace is With All Already

The very last verse in the Bible (Revelation 22:21) says, "The grace of the Lord Jesus be with all. Amen."

In the original Greek, it actually reads, "Grace (our Lord Jesus Christ) is face to face with all" (every, any, all, the whole, everyone, all things, everything). *Jesus* is with *all*, and *Jesus is Grace!*

Look at what Paul wrote to the church in Rome: Romans 5:15–17 (Parenthesis and italics mine): "The free gift (Jesus who is Grace) is not like the transgression. For if by the transgression of the one the many died, much more did the *grace of God* and the *gift by the grace of the one Man, Jesus Christ,* abound to the many. *The gift* (Jesus who is Grace) is not like *that which came* through the one who sinned; for on the one hand the judgment *arose* from one *transgression* resulting in condemnation, but on the other hand the *free gift (Jesus who is Grace) arose* from many transgressions resulting in justification. For if by the transgression of the one, death reigned through the one, much more those who *receive the abundance of grace (Jesus)* and of the *gift of righteousness* will reign in life through the One, Jesus Christ."

Listen carefully: the enemy/deceiver/liar has kept us in the dark *and ripped us off.* When we hear about grace, righteousness, free gift, fullness, etc., he tells us that those are things ('doctrines,' 'concepts,' 'nebulous mystical spiritual deals'). He says, "You can't really define or understand them, but you must work hard to achieve them." Those are all lies!

Here is the truth that will open your eyes and set you free from the darkness—God the Father is the giver, and *Jesus Christ is the gift! Jesus is grace!*

You and I, and everyone, were given the greatest gift of all time at the cross. We were given *Jesus Christ, Grace Himself* who came to live in us!

Colossians 1:27 says, "This is the mystery: Christ in you, the Hope of Glory!"

a 'Potential Gift'

...at the original definition of *grace* meant *a birth-*
...postle John knew that meaning when he wrote:
...loved the world, that He gave His only begotten Son,
that ...oever believes in Him shall not perish, but have eternal
life" (John 3:16).

A tremendous amount of thought went into that gift. Remember the concept was that what the gift was worth indicated the value or worth that the giver placed on the person receiving the gift.

God—Jesus, Papa, and the Holy Spirit—knew you and chose you before creation. They loved you unconditionally before They created you. They wanted to give you a birthday gift—a *grace* that showed you how much They valued you.

They could have just given you the gift of life …

They could have just given you freedom from the law …

They could have just given you spiritual gifts … like leadership or speaking in tongues …

They could have just forgiven your sins …

Those are all nice, wonderful, stupendous! But They wanted to give you something that would show exactly how much They valued you.

So, *They gave you the most valuable entity in the entire universe—They gave you Jesus Himself! Jesus, Grace, is the gift! Grace is in you!*

2 Timothy 1:9–10 (Italics mine): "God has saved us and called *us* with a holy calling, not according to our works, but according to *His own purpose and grace which was given to us in Christ Jesus before time began* but has now *been revealed by the appearing of our Savior Jesus Christ, who* has abolished death and brought life and immortality to light through the gospel."

Because of God's great love for you, He gave you the greatest gift ever. Not a potential gift. Not something you have to do something to get. God gave Jesus to you before creation, and then in time and space, at the cross, He put Him in you. The Holy Spirit of Christ is in you right now.

Who Are You Going To Believe?

John 3:16 says, "God so loved the world, that He gave His only begotten Son, that whoever believes in Him shall not perish, but have eternal life."

You may be perishing right now. You may perish tonight. The Greek word that we translate 'perish' means 'to destroy, render useless, to be lost.' Who wants to destroy you?

John 10:10 (Jesus): "The thief comes only to steal and kill and destroy, but I come to give you life!"

There are two different entities who are extremely interested in you. Jesus, who loves you unconditionally, has forgiven you completely, who is for you, and who *IS* Grace ... and the thief/evil one/liar/deceiver who is totally against you.

The Father gave us Jesus so that we wouldn't perish but have eternal/everlasting life which is right here and now ... and forever!

Every day and every moment, we have the opportunity to believe one of those entities. Do you believe what the Spirit is saying to you ... or do you believe the lie of evil?

The Truth is that Jesus Christ, God Himself, pure grace, the gift of God ... is in you, and He is for you! Christ in you, the hope of glory!

And here's what He wants: He wants to live as you and through you. When He does, grace is multiplied all over the earth.

When you choose Jesus, which means to choose to let Him live as you and through you instead of believing lies, you don't perish—you thrive, you experience and enjoy abundant eternal everlasting life!

Jesus, who knows everything, who is all powerful and is everywhere present, lives in you and wants to express Himself as you and through you.

Expressing Himself looks like unconditional love for you and everyone you come in contact with, total forgiveness, universal acceptance and inclusion, joy, peace, patience, kindness, goodness, gentleness, faith, mercy, and grace.

When that happens, you will literally be radiant and overflowing with joy. People will be attracted to you.

You Are Attractive!

If no one is noticing that there's something different about you, then they're not seeing Jesus. I'm not saying that in a condemning way; I'm saying that in a positive, hopeful way to encourage you to choose to let Jesus live as you and through you. That's a win, win, win situation for everyone.

That's grace multiplied … abounding grace … hyper grace— grace upon grace! The New Covenant of Grace Himself is *in* you!

Ephesians 1:17 (MIRROR): "I desire that you will draw directly from the source; that the God of our Lord Jesus Christ, the Father of glory ignites the spirit of wisdom and of revelation in you in the unveiling of his Master Plan. I desire that you know by revelation what He has known about you all along!"

Ephesians 4:15 (MIRROR) (Italics mine): "Love gives truth its voice. The conversation that truth inspires creates the atmosphere wherein growth is both spontaneous and inevitable. The whole person is addressed in Christ who is the head of the body; he is the conclusion of God's communication with man."

NLT: "Instead, we will speak the truth in love, *growing in every way more and more like Christ*, who is the head of his body, the church."

Ephesians 4:16 (MIRROR): "From Him flows the original composition and detail of our design like words intertwined in poetry, (like a conductor of music) they connect layer upon layer to complete the harmony, following the rhythm of His thoughts like footprints. Meanwhile the body thrives and pulsates with the energy of love. Each individual expression finds its complete measure there."

Philippians 1:9 (MIRROR): "It is my desire for each one of you, that the realization of love's completeness in you will increasingly burst through all boundaries, and that every sphere of your relationship with others will be greatly impacted by your intimate acquaintance with love."

Colossians 1:6 (MIRROR): "This word resonates within you and its appeal is prevailing in the whole world. The harvest is evident everywhere and gaining ground; as also witnessed in your own experience from the moment you heard and understood the true implication and the relevance of His grace … You continue to increase in your intimate acquaintance with that which God knows to be true about you. This results in the most attractive and fulfilled life possible."

People are Attracted to Christ

The most attractive and fulfilled life possible is the life of grace! The most attractive and fulfilled life ever in history was Jesus's life. More people have been attracted to Jesus and His life than anyone ever in the history of the world.

People are attracted to other people because of their success. We're attracted to successful athletes. We identify with them and want to be like them. They inspire us. Children *and* adults imagine we're like them. Remember the Michael Jordan slogan, "Be like Mike!" We're attracted to successful artists, musicians, actors, writers, and composers. They inspire us; they make us feel like we're part of something grand, something bigger than just ourselves.

In all of these instances, the person that is attractive to us has accomplished something magnificent ... they may still be plying their craft, but they have successfully finished something, whether it's a sport's championship or title, a piece of art or musical composition or performance recording, a film or story ... they have successfully finished something.

Jesus is attractive to us not just because of His miracles, not just because of His wise teaching, not just because of His love, forgiveness, acceptance, and inclusion of everyone, and not just because of His rising from the dead.

Jesus is *most attractive* because *He finished something!* Not just *something*, but *the most important thing ever!*

Jesus defeated death, sin, and evil forever. Jesus took away all the sin of the world forever. Jesus died once for all. Jesus included all of mankind forever in His crucifixion, death, burial, resurrection, and ascension. Everyone died with Jesus, and Jesus gave everyone life. Jesus made everyone new creations. The Holy Spirit of Christ took up residence in each of us permanently.

Jesus finished God's work for Him at the cross!

Hebrews 12:2 says, "So now we fix our eyes on Jesus, the author and perfecter of faith, who for the joy set before Him endured the cross, despising the shame, and has sat down at the right hand of the throne of God."

Ephesians 2:8–9 (MIRROR): "Your salvation is not a reward

for good behavior! It was a grace thing from start to finish; you had no hand in it. Even the gift to believe simply reflects His (Christ's) faith! (By grace you are! Saved by the gift of faith; grace reveals who we are, and the faith of God persuades us of it! You did not invent faith; it was God's faith to begin with! It is from faith to faith, (Romans 1:17) He is both the source and conclusion of faith.) (Hebrews 12:2) If this could be accomplished through any action of yours then there would be ground for boasting."

Restored

2 Peter 2:1–11 (MIRROR): "I am Simon the Rock, bondman and ambassador of Jesus Christ. We are in this together; God's faith sees everyone equally valued and justified in Jesus Christ our Savior. God's desire is that we may now increasingly be overwhelmed with grace as His divine influence within us and become fully acquainted with the awareness of our oneness. The way He has always known us is realized in Jesus our Master.

"By His divine engineering He gifted us with all that it takes to live life to the full, where our ordinary day to day lives mirror our devotion and romance with our Maker. His intimate knowledge of us introduces us to ourselves again and elevates us to a position where his original intention is clearly perceived!

"This is exactly what God always had in mind for us; every one of His abundant and priceless promises pointed to our restored participation in our godly origin! This is His gift to us! In this fellowship, we have escaped the distorted influence of the corrupt cosmic virus of greed.

"Now (in the light of what we are gifted with in Christ) the stage is set to display life's excellence. Explore the adventure of faith! Imagine the extreme dedication and focus of a conductor of music; how he would diligently acquaint himself with every individual voice in the choir, as well as the contribution of every specific instrument, to follow the precise sound represented in every single note in order to give maximum credit to the original composition. This is exactly what it means to exhibit the divine character. You are the choir conductor of your own life. Study the full content of faith; discover in faith how elevated you are, and from within this position (of your co-seatedness in Christ), enlightened perspective will dawn within you.

"Here you will realize your inner strength and how fully competent you are to prevail in patient perseverance in the midst of any contradiction. It is from within this place of enlightened perspective that meaningful devotion and worship ignite!

"In worship you will find a genuine fondness for others. At

the heart of everything that faith unfolds is the agape-love of God. While you diligently rehearse the exact qualities of every divine attribute within you; the volume will rise with ever increasing gusto, guarding you from being ineffective and barren in your knowledge of the Christ-life, displayed with such authority and eloquence in Jesus."

The Great Conductor

2 Peter 1:9–11 (MIRROR): "If anyone feels that these things are absent in his life, they are not; spiritual blindness and short-sightedness only veil them from you. This happens when one loses sight of one's innocence. (The moment one forgets the tremendous consequence of the fact that we were cleansed from our past sins, one seems to become pre-occupied again with the immediate sense-ruled horizon, which is what short-sightedness is all about; this makes one blind to his blessings. Spiritual realities suddenly seem vague and distant. Become acquainted with your innocence!)

"Therefore I would encourage you my fellow family, to make every immediate effort to become cemented in the knowledge of our original identity revealed and confirmed in the logic of God. Fully engage these realities in your lifestyle, and so you will never fail. Thus, the great Conductor of music will draw your life into the full volume of the harmony of the ages; the royal song of our Savior Jesus Christ."

1 John 4:17 (MIRROR): "So now, with us awakening to our full inclusion in this love union, everything is perfect! Its completeness is not compromised in contradiction. Our confident conversation echoes this fellowship even in the face of crisis; because as He is, so are we in this world– our lives are mirrored in Him!"

Colossians 2:7, 2:19 (MIRROR): "Just like the roots of a tree, draw your sustenance and strength from Him. Like a building rising up out of its foundation your life makes the full stature of Christ visible; standing tall in His shoes, firm in your faith posture. The language of gratitude that overflows from your lips reflects the exact impression of what you were taught… religious jargon is completely out of rhythm with the head. You are directly connected to Christ who like a choir conductor draws out the music in everyone like a tapestry of art that intertwines in harmony to reveal the full stature of divine inspiration (which is Christ in you)."

1 Thessalonians 3:12 says, "And may the Lord make your love for one another and for all people grow and overflow, just as our love for you overflows."

2 Thessalonians 1:3 says, "We ought always to give thanks to God for you, brethren, as is *only* fitting, because your faith is greatly enlarged, and the love of each one of you toward one another grows *ever* greater."

2 Peter 3:18 says, "but grow in the grace and knowledge of our Lord and Savior Jesus Christ. To Him *be* the glory both now and forever. Amen."

Zechariah 4:6–7 (Italics mine): "Then he said to me, 'This is the word of the LORD to Zerubbabel saying, "Not by might nor by power, but by My Spirit," says the LORD of hosts. "What are you, O great mountain? Before Zerubbabel *you will become* a plain; and he will bring forth the top stone with shouts of *Grace, grace to it!*"'"

Author Steve McVey posted this wonderful article at www.stevemcvey.com:

Do Grace and Truth Need to Be Kept in Balance?
June 2, 2016 Steve McVey

The assertion that grace and truth need to be kept in balance is one of the predictable objections to the undiluted message of God's grace. This lie is particularly dangerous because the concept of balance in life is so prevalent and in many cases, correct. For example, finding balance between work and leisure is a good thing. Finding a balance between saving money and hoarding is important. The list could go on, but the idea of balance doesn't apply in every way imaginable. For instance, finding a balance between fidelity and infidelity in marriage makes no sense. Sometimes the attempt to apply the concept of balance simply doesn't fit. That's the case when it comes to truth and grace.

Nobody who takes the Bible seriously can deny its teaching about grace. At the same time, there are those who struggle with the pure, undiluted grace of God, so they take the concept of balance and try to apply it here. They can't very well deny the grace of God—it's too evident in Scripture. But they'll try to tone it down with this argument: "Well, yes," they say. "Grace is a wonderful truth. But you have to keep grace and truth in balance with each other so you don't go to an extreme." Since few people want to be "extreme," that seems to make reasonable sense.

This approach is problematic because it draws a line down the middle and puts grace on one side and truth on the other, as if the two are in opposition to each other. It's as if they're saying that grace is not truth and truth is not grace. That's not what the Bible says. Grace and truth do not stand in contrast to each other. The Bible puts grace and truth on the same side of the line. Grace is truth, and the truth is grace. To separate them as I've described is a legalistic way to interpret God's grace.

The Truth Is So Much Better!

Does the Bible teach a balance between grace and truth as though the two are separate realities? It does not. To the contrary, Scripture inseparably joins the two together in the person of Jesus Christ. The Bible says, "The Law was given through Moses; grace and truth were realized through Jesus Christ" (John 1:17).

John says here that grace and truth came to fullness (to fruition) in the person of Jesus Christ. He wasn't part grace and part truth. He was 100 percent grace and 100 percent truth! You can find the qualities of both in Christ. They're in perfect harmony and unity. All by itself, John 1:17 proves that grace and truth are not opposed to one another.

If you're going to draw a line, draw it between grace and legalism—not between grace and truth. The Bible plainly puts grace and truth on the same side of the line, in Jesus. So anytime you hear people say, "Well, this message of grace is good, but you have to balance that with truth," you can recognize what they are doing. Whether they are sincerely mistaken or committed legalists, you can know that it's a lie, because grace and truth are not on two different sides of the dividing line. They're on the same side of the line. Legalism is on the other side of the line. Grace and truth are synonymous because they are expressed (or personified) in the person of Jesus Christ, who is "full of grace and truth."

Why do we struggle so much with this? Admittedly, human

beings often aren't in balance. We do tend to lean toward different extremes. But let's not confuse this matter of grace and truth. Grace and truth are in perfect harmony. There's nothing to balance between them. They're perfectly complementary.

Clarify Your Thinking.

The lie that we need to find a balance between grace and truth might sound good to those who don't know better, but I can't overstate the devastating effect of attempting to divide the two. Grace and truth are conjoined twins. You cannot separate them without killing both.

To suggest that we should find balance within the topic of grace is an insidious lie. Any attempt to do that is to compromise grace. Grace is Jesus, and He doesn't need to be balanced with anything. Balance Him with truth? Reject that nonsense. He is truth!

Whether they know it or not, people who say that we need to maintain a balance in the teaching of grace are suggesting that it needs to be watered down so that it's not so offensive to the legalist. Remember, the legalist feels like there must be something that we have to contribute to this life we have received in Christ. But as we've discussed, you can't add anything. You already have Jesus, and He is grace and truth—the whole truth and nothing but the truth.

CHAPTER 4
GLORY IS GOD'S GRACE

What Mr. Wiley Was All About

How would you describe yourself? Are there one or two words or phrases that would really capture who you are?

The opinion we have of ourselves … the way we describe ourselves … might not be the way others would describe us. It might not be the way God describes us, either!

My University band director, Russell Wiley, served at the University of Kansas for over 40 years. He was a very accomplished musician, top-flight conductor, amazing recruiter, super innovator, highly creative and highly decorated. People used all these and a plethora of other highly complementary ways to describe him.

However, to find out what he was really like, who he really was, what motivated him, you needed to spend time with him—know him personally and observe him in action.

But to really find out who he was at his core … you needed to listen to what he had to say about himself, what was important to him, what he dedicated his life to.

One summer when I was working for Mr. Wiley, he had just dismissed one of his peers from another prestigious university … a man who seemed to 'bask in his own glory,' as he was appearing as a guest conductor at Mr. Wiley's summer camp for high school musicians. This other conductor had publicly humiliated a student for the quality of instrument his parents had provided him with. Without making a scene, Mr. Wiley privately paid the man and gave him a one-way plane ticket home.

In explaining the situation to me, he related that what he was all about was building up and encouraging students to be all they could be. He wanted to empower kids and give them confidence and help them reach musical heights they never imagined. His help didn't stop with the band. He got students like me jobs, he opened doors for non-music major kids to get accepted into other programs, and he used his considerable influence to help students after college.

He described himself as helping people become all they could be. Music just happened to be the tool he had with which to do that.

Once when I was working for him, I really let him down by forgetting about an important responsibility I had. He ended up doing the work for me. Afterward, he knew that *I knew* he had personally done my work. Do you know what he said to me about how I let him down and he had to do my work? Nothing. Ever. He gave me grace. For all his accomplishments, awards and acclaim, I realized that his 'glory' was his grace.

Describing God

How would you describe God? People usually use the word *glory* to describe God.

The New Testament Greek word that we translate 'glory' is 'doxa,' which literally means 'opinion of.' The Glory of God means two things: 1st, God's opinion of Himself—who He thinks He really is, what He's all about. 2nd, God's opinion of mankind, what He thinks about us, who He thinks we really are.

Seminary students are taught that glory (doxa: opinion) means 'everything about a person'—their reputation, their recognition, their fame, what they are praised and honored for, what distinguishes them, all that comprises them, their splendor.

They are taught the 'characteristics of God's glory,' starting with the Three Big O's:

Omnipotent– God is all-powerful.

Omniscient– God is all-knowing; He knows everything.

Omnipresent– God is everywhere present at the same time.

We sometimes describe God's Glory in terms of Him being the Creator …we look at majestic mountains, ocean coastlines and beautify scenery that God created, and we talk about His glory.

In the Old Testament, the Jewish people talked about His glory when He would save them and punish their enemies … who, of course, were God's enemies (or were they?).

I was taught (maybe you were, too) that you should fear God … be afraid of Him because He knew all your thoughts … everything you did, He was always there watching you, and He was all powerful. He was keeping a list of the bad things I did, and I would have to pay for them and His punishment because He was all-powerful; there would be hell to pay.

I was taught that God punished bad people forever … *really* punished them … in hell.

However, to find out what God is actually like, perhaps we should spend time with Him … and ask Him.

God Describes Himself as 'Grace'

If you were to ask God how He would describe Himself—what exactly is His glory—what would He say? We don't have to wonder; Moses asked Him!

God had Moses set up a tent (a mobile tabernacle) where God would meet with Moses in the desert where they were after crossing the Red Sea.

Exodus 33:11–19 (Italics mine): "The LORD spoke to Moses face to face, as a man speaks to his friend. Then Moses said to the LORD: 'You have said, "I know you by name, and you have also *found grace* in My sight." Now therefore, I pray, if I have *found* grace in Your sight, show me now Your way, that I may know You and that I may *find grace* in Your sight.' So the LORD said to Moses, 'I will also do this thing that you have spoken; for *you have found grace* in My sight, and I know you by name.'

"And Moses said, 'Please, *show me Your glory.*' Then the Lord said, 'I will make all *My goodness* pass before you, and I will proclaim the name of the LORD before you. *I will be gracious to whom I will be gracious, and I will have compassion on whom I will have compassion.*'"

Be sure that you get the main points of this: Moses *found grace in God's sight*; God knew him personally; Moses asked to see God's glory, and God said, "OK, I will show you my *goodness.* I will *be gracious,* I will give *grace* and compassion on whoever I want!"

God Himself, when asked to *show His glory* to us, *showed us His goodness—expressed as His grace.*

Exactly how He showed Moses His goodness and Grace, we don't know ... but we know that *God considers His glory to be His goodness and His grace.*

Jesus, who is God and who is Grace, who is glorious in every imaginable way, considers His glory to be *His Grace!*

nsiders His Glory to Be His Grace

ı search the entire Bible, in addition to Exodus 33, you   only one other place in the Bible that specifically describes God's glory. The Apostle Paul, who had been taken by Jesus up to 'The Third Heaven,' wrote the following:

Ephesians 1:2–6 (Italics and parenthesis mine) "*Grace* to you and peace from God our Father and the Lord Jesus Christ. Blessed *be* the God and Father of our Lord Jesus Christ, who has blessed us with every spiritual blessing in the heavenly *places* in Christ, just as He chose us in Him before the foundation of the world, that we should be holy and without blame before Him in love, having predestined us to adoption as sons by Jesus Christ to Himself, according to the good pleasure of His will, (remember God told Moses that He would be gracious to whomever He wanted). Because of God's love for us, He chose us all before creation, blessed us with every spiritual blessing there is, put us in Christ, made us holy and without blame before him, adopted us into His family– this was His will and it gave Him good pleasure!) 'to the praise of the *glory of His grace,* by which He made us accepted in the Beloved.'"

God did all of this and made us accepted in Christ … to the praise of the *glory of His grace.* God Himself considers His glory to be His GRACE!

Glory (Opinion). God's opinion of Himself is His Grace!

Of all the things God could talk about … all of His power and knowledge and ability, what God considers most important in His opinion of Himself *is His Grace!*

If you love someone unconditionally … even when they are unlovable … what do you call that? Grace! If you forgive someone over and over again, no matter how many times they hurt you or offend you, what do you call that? *Grace*! If you are good to someone who doesn't deserve for you to be good to them, what is that called? *Grace*! If you are patient with someone who is slow and not catching on and can't seem to get it right, what is that called? *Grace*! If you are peaceful even when those around you are full of strife, bitterness, and are loud, complaining and obnoxious, that called? *Grace*!

You know what it takes to give grace in all those situations? Supernatural power.

God is all-powerful. And instead of using His power to strike back, to be harsh, to punish … He demonstrates His power by giving grace instead of what we would expect. That is His Glory!

Jesus Considers His Glory to Be His Grace

You can sing about God's glory, and you can use the word glory to praise Him, but you can't grasp or understand God's glory—His love and compassion and goodness and grace—except as it reaches out to and touches you personally and those you are with.

The glory of God is understood in the truth that He totally gives Himself away! At the heart of the glory of God is Grace!

God is the original definer of 'give,' and it's not just that He gives to us—He actually *is* 'giving-ness.' Giving is who He is.

Everything God does is good. Jesus Himself is a gift to us … He is both the giver and the gift!

God, the creator of everything, pours His glory into you and me … all of us. He is kind, gentle, patient, good, faithful, joyful and peaceful to you, me, and everyone. He loves us all unconditionally. That is glory, His Glory. He is glorious!

John 1:14 (Italics mine): "And the Word (Jesus) became flesh and dwelt among us, and *we beheld His glory*, the glory as of the only begotten of the Father, full of grace and truth."

John said that they beheld—they first-hand witnessed *Jesus's glory—and it was His grace and truth!* We're Christians, and we're told the goal is to be like Jesus. My understanding is that we're to be full of (which we are!) and give Grace!

Being like Jesus is not having perfect church attendance. It's not memorizing the Bible. It's not serving at the soup kitchen. It's not tithing. It's not being morally perfect.

Being like Jesus is letting Christ Jesus, in you, live His life as you and through you. When you do, it looks like unconditionally loving and forgiving people in your life, no matter if they deserve it or not. It's having His joy and having His attitude.

Being like Jesus is having His peace, maintaining peace. It's having His patience, having His kindness. That's being glorious. That's Jesus's glory … His Grace!

Christ in You—The Hope of Glory

I want you to see why learning that God's glory is actually His grace is way more than just a theology lesson.

Stuff happens in our lives. Bad stuff. Doesn't it? We get taken advantage of; we get lied to. People offend us. They hurt us. They abuse us. Unfair things happen. Our loved ones aren't faithful.

Now be honest; when someone hurts you, what do we want to happen to them? While we might not admit it out loud, most of us want them to get caught, to be embarrassed and ashamed. We want them to pay for their wrong. We want them to be punished.

Take that a step further. When people do bad things to us or others, we want God to get them. We want Him to make them pay. We want Him to smite them, curse them, harm them.

We want God to vindicate us, announce that we are right and we are the victims; thus, they are in the wrong.

We want other people to get what they deserve … from God.

We want God to bless us … and curse them.

And how you and I want God to treat other people is usually going to be how *we* treat them.

I used to talk about people from other religions or about atheists or about people who said that God was different than *I* thought He was, and I used to say to my friends, "They're going to get a rude awakening when they die and see God face to face … they're going to get what they deserve!" Of course, that's what I wanted to happen. I thought, *Hell is the ultimate punishment. They deserve it. I hope they'll burn in hell.* Have you ever said or thought that about someone?

We know that God is all-powerful. We believe in Him. We're 'Christians.' So how do we want Him to use His power in regard to those who hurt us … those who are different from us … those whose lifestyle disgusts us? These are questions we really should be asking. The Holy Spirit has revealed to me that God, Christ in me, wants to treat other people just like He treats me and you. He wants to do that *AS* you and me, and through you and me … *so that other people can experience the glory of God!*

Christ in you, the hope of glory!

Grace Is With You In Good Times And Bad

Religion tells us that God loves those who keep the rules, who do good, who are 'holy and righteous, good Christians.' Religion says that God's glory is His power that comes against people who don't measure up to His standards.

But God says that His glory is that He loves people who *don't* keep the rules, who *don't* do good, who *aren't* 'good Christians!' That's how He demonstrates His power!

We all want God's unconditional love for us. We all want God to forgive us unconditionally. We all want God's grace for us.

Wanting God's grace for everyone is what Christ in you wants. Christ in you, the hope of glory!

Let's look at God's glory, His grace to us and in us, when something bad in our life happens that is not caused by another person.

Cancer happens ... so does premature death, disabilities, debilitating injuries. The economy changes, and there is no longer need for what we're good at. Those things happen. We've had bad things happen to our family where there's not another person to blame. Bad stuff happens because we live in a fallen world.

Think for a moment—is there a situation in your life right now, or in the life of a close friend or family member, that's not good, not fair? Where does God's grace, His glory, come in there?

The biggest thing, and I think the most important thing, is that in those times, God is with us. Don't ever trivialize that. No matter how bad something is, God, Jesus, is with you. He's in you, and He's empowering you. That is not a trite, insignificant thing. Yes, your situation is tragic. It's awful. You can't see anything good in it. But Jesus is with you, and He can totally relate to you because of what happened to Him at the cross.

He is with you, and He will go through it with you. He and His grace will ultimately be sufficient. You will realize that He is enough. If all that ever happened to you was good stuff, you could believe God is good, but you'd never understand personally how He is good to those who go through bad times ... until you experience it yourself.

God Gives Grace Through You

When you're at your lowest, and you don't know how you can go on ... when you hurt so bad, and you've cried so much that your tear ducts are dry ... you can't even cry any more ... when that one relationship that was more important to you than any other is no more ... when you used to be vibrant and healthy, and that's gone ... when you are so sad that words can't describe it ...

Jesus says, "I know. I'm here. I hurt with you. I'm sad too. And I'm with you. I'm in you, and I'll never leave you or forsake you. My grace is sufficient. You can't see it right now, but I promise you that it is. My glory is my compassion and grace nurturing you, comforting you and empowering you right now.

"You can do this through Me, and I will be your strength. I am the Rock, and I will be *your* Rock. I am your Rock.

"And most importantly ... as bad as this is, there is coming a day when I will make it right. You will be whole and healthy and so will all your loved ones. I am making all things right for everyone. Every wrong will be made right. There will be no more pain, no more sickness, no more grief, no more sin, no more inequality, no more injustice ... there will be true justice—Me making everything right for everyone."

That's what you can expect to hear from Jesus in the worst moments of your life. He wants you to get to know Him now and learn to hear His voice now and learn what He's like now and experience His grace and glory now ... so that you can more easily recognize and experience it in your time of deepest need.

Jesus is Grace. God's glory is His Grace.

You know when we meet new people, the question inevitably gets around to: "So what do you do?" I think if someone were to meet Jesus for the first time and asked Him what does He do, He might say: "I give grace."

Christ/Grace is in you, the Hope of Glory!

As you get to know Him more, you most likely will also hear Him say, "Now I'd like to start giving grace *AS* you and through you to everyone you're with!"

Jesus Voted For You

Remember the last U.S. presidential election? Supporters of each candidate were trying to convince undecided people to vote for their candidate. They gave new information about their person—they touted the selling points of their candidate. They stated what he or she was for and against.

They paint the picture that the country is in dire trouble and only their candidate can fix the trouble and make things right. They tout their accomplishments and background and make a case that they can get the job done.

We're not in an election for God or for Jesus. We're not trying to get people to vote for Jesus. Jesus already voted for us, and that's the only vote that counts!

However, the situation is that Jesus is the only one who can ultimately make a difference in people's lives both right now and in the future in the next life … and forever! The situation also is that most people, even Christians, have no idea what Jesus, God, is like. They have vague, usually incorrect ideas about His nature, His glory.

Here's where we come in. What if you and I let Jesus live His life of love and grace not only in us but as us and through us so that He can give grace to everyone in our lives every day as we go about our lives? And what if we intentionally make it a point to tell other people that Jesus is GRACE and explain a little bit about what that means to us?

Jesus will actually do the talking. That's when it gets to be really fun and really helpful to other people. Here's how Paul put it when he encouraged some people to do just that:

Philemon 6 (NKJV): "The sharing of your faith will become effective by the acknowledgment of every good thing which is in you in Christ Jesus."

Ephesians 1:17 (MIRROR): "I desire that you will draw directly from the Source, that the God of our Lord Jesus Christ, The Father of Glory, ignites the Spirit of wisdom and of revelation in you in the unveiling of His master plan.

I desire that you know by revelation what He has known about you all along!"

Grace To You

I encourage you today to take some time and ask the Holy Spirit of Christ to remind you of times in your past where another person gave you grace.

Ask God to bring to mind a situation or circumstance where you hurt someone ... intentionally or unintentionally. Maybe it's a time where you gossiped or slandered a friend. Maybe you took credit at work for something they did. Maybe there was a time in your life when you betrayed a confidence or betrayed a friend or took advantage of someone inappropriately. Perhaps there was a time when you could have helped someone, you could have righted a wrong, you could have validated something, you could have stopped an injustice ... but you didn't. Maybe you actually cheated someone ... a business partner or relative or friend ... or spouse.

Let the Holy Spirit bring one (or more) of those situations to your mind. He will never do that in a condemning, shaming or accusatory way. God actually chooses to forget our sins and trespasses and chooses not to bring them up to us or hold them against us. However, when we ask Him for the purpose of showing us His grace and glory, I've found that He will honor our request.

Remember, now, how you felt when you hurt someone, they knew you hurt them, and they forgave you unconditionally, continued to love you unconditionally, continued to accept and include you ... when you didn't deserve it at all. That is GRACE. That is glorious.

That's how Jesus, Papa, and the Holy Spirit always relate to you. When someone else relates to you like that, whether they know it or not, that is Christ in them ... the Hope of Glory!

As you revel and bask in the Glory of God's grace and love, now let Him do what He wants. Christ in you wants to love and give grace to everyone in your life as you and through you. When He does, you, the recipients and everyone watching experience, enjoy and marvel at His Glory!

Ephesians 4:29 says, "Let no corrupt communication proceed

out of your mouth, but only that which is good to the use of edifying and building others up, that it may minister grace unto the hearers."

(MIRROR): "Instead of cheap talk, your mouth is now a fountain of grace, giving encouragement and inspiration to everyone within earshot."

CHAPTER 5
JESUS'S FINISHED WORK
FOR ALL MANKIND

Good News: Jesus Finished It All

Just before Jesus died on the cross, He said, "It is finished" (Greek: "Tetelestai" —John 19:30).

Hebrews 4:10 (MIRROR): "God's rest celebrates His finished work; whoever enters into God's rest immediately abandons his own efforts to compliment what God has already perfected. (The language of the law is 'do;' the language of grace is 'done.')"

Jesus, Papa, and the Holy Spirit working together, actually finished everything necessary for all people in our relationship with God! Just because very few people are aware of that great Truth of all Truths doesn't mean it's not true!

Many people have believed religion's lie that those are potential truths that are *conditionally* available only after they do some *required* thing. That, of course, leads to great uncertainty and much confusion. People wonder, *Have I done enough? Did I do it right? Was I sincere? Have I done something to negate what I previously did? Did I miss anything?* However, Jesus seems to think He did it all for us in His finished work at the cross!

There is literally nothing left, nothing necessary, nothing that we can or must do to *get right with God.* They didn't leave anything up to chance ... they took care of it all.

I know this is different, contrary to what you probably have been taught and believed. It was certainly news to me, even after I'd been a 'Christian' for almost 20 years!

Think of how your life can change if you know and are confident that God loved you so much that He took no chances and proactively did everything (at great cost!) to ensure your inclusion not only into His family but into Their Divine Triune circle dance of love and everything good that flows from Their love: joy, peace, patience, kindness, goodness, gentleness, faith, self-control, compassion, mercy, grace, and so much more!

Human failure in every tense and sense of the word was dealt with in Jesus's death, burial, and resurrection!

Jesus wants you to have complete and total assurance ... so He did it all. We call that *Good News!*

Jesus's Finished Work Is All Important

I don't believe it's an understatement at all to say that grasping the revelation of Jesus's finished work at the cross for *all* mankind is the most important thing of all in our relationship with God!

Jesus's finished work demonstrates once and for all that God is love, God is obsessed with community with us, God's grace has taken care of everything for us in our relationship with God, and God has included and accepted everyone in their family in Christ!

Only when we *believe* that Jesus's work at the cross finished *everything* for us to be right with God both now and forever can we relax and rest in our relationship with God, all others, and ourselves!

Hebrews 3:8–19 (MIRROR): "Do not be calloused in heart as the people of Israel were: every time they faced any contradiction or temptation in the wilderness, their response immediately revealed their irritation rather than their persuasion in God's belief. Your fathers continued to scrutinize Me suspiciously, examining Me as though My intentions with them could not be trusted, even though they were eye-witnesses of My miraculous works for forty years.

"They were a generation of people who grieved Me deeply; instead of learning My ways, they habitually went astray in their hearts, intoxicated by their unbelief. Hear the echo of God's cry through the ages, 'Oh! If only they would enter into My rest.'

"Make sure that none of you tolerates the poison of unbelief in your hearts, allowing callousness to distract and distance you from the living God. (Unbelief is believing a lie about yourself and your salvation. Unbelief exchanges the living God for a dead god of your own imagination. A calloused heart is a mind dominated by the senses.)

"Instead, remind one another daily of your true identity. Who we are in our union with Christ must be taken to its ultimate conclusion … God's invitation does not exclude anyone from possessing the promise of His rest; their unbelief does. Persuasion cannot be compromised by unbelief. They failed to grasp what God had in mind for them.

"The ultimate proof of faith is not experience of the supernatural, but entering into His rest. His rest celebrates His perfect work (at the cross)."

Hebrews 5:14 says, "This is the nourishment of the mature. They are those who have their faculties of perception trained as by gymnastic precision to distinguish the relevant from the irrelevant. (The mature are those who know the difference between the shadow and the substance; between the futility of the law of works and willpower to work righteousness, and righteousness revealed by the faith of God in the finished work of Christ!)"

Good News: The Cross Was a Success

From Francois du Toit, *Introduction to Hebrews* in the *Mirror Bible:*

"In the Gospel, the righteousness of God is revealed, from faith to faith (Romans 1:17). Herein lies the secret of the power of the Gospel; there is no good news in it until the righteousness of God is revealed!

"(The good news is the fact that the cross of Christ was a success. God rescued the life of our design; He redeemed our innocence. Mankind would never again be judged righteous or unrighteous by their own ability to obey moral laws! It is not about what a person must or must not do, but about what Jesus has done!)

"God now persuades everyone to believe what He knows to be true about them. (It is from faith to faith.) The prophets wrote in advance about the fact that God believes that righteousness unveils the life that He always had in mind for us. 'The just shall live by His (God's) faith.' Righteousness by God's faith defines life.

"The Gospel is the revelation of the righteousness of God; it declares how God succeeded to put mankind right with Him. It is about what God did right, not what Adam did wrong. The word righteousness comes from the Anglo-Saxon word 'rightwiseness,' meaning wise in that which is right. In Greek, the word for righteousness is 'dikaiosune' from 'dike,' which means two parties finding likeness in each other.

"If Christ is both the author and perfecter of faith, self-assessment by any other reference would be foolish. It would be just as impossible to attempt to measure temperature with a ruler. Christ defines our original design and our restored innocence. We find our identity and our destiny there.

"We have obtained unrestricted access into the intimate and immediate friendship of God! A brand-new way of life has been introduced!"

Jesus Did It All—For All

Jesus accomplished *everything* by His finished work at the cross. Because of what Jesus did for us in His death, burial, resurrection, ascension, and pouring out His Holy Spirit on us, we do not have to strive or work to 'become like Christ.' We don't have to work to maintain a right standing with God or to earn or keep His favor. He has done all that for us in advance! It is finished!

All were included IN Christ!

Jesus took away all the sin of all the world!

God reconciled all the world to Himself!

We all died with Jesus—Adam's entire race died!

All rose with Jesus—God gave us new life in Christ, who is the last Adam!

All were born again at resurrection!

All were made pure, holy, righteous, innocent, without fault, and perfect!

The Holy Spirit was poured out on all people!

All were hidden with God in Christ!

All were raised to the heavenly realms and seated with Christ!

All Means All

Jesus began everything. He's the beginning. He's the one that spoke everything into existence. He's in all, through all, for all. Everything was created by Him.

John 1:3 (Italics mine): "*All* things were made through Him, and without Him nothing was made that was made."

1 Corinthians 15:22 (Italics mine): "For as in Adam *all* die, even so in Christ *all* shall be made alive."

Ephesians 4:4–6 (Italics mine): "*There is* one body and one Spirit, just as you were called in one hope of your calling; one Lord, one faith, one baptism; one God and Father of all, who *is* above *all*, and through *all*, and in *all*."

Colossians 3:11 (Italics mine): "There is neither Greek *nor* Jew, circumcised nor uncircumcised, barbarian, Scythian, slave nor free, but Christ *is all* and *in all*."

1 Peter 3:18 says, "For Christ also suffered once for sins, the just for the unjust, that He might bring us to God, being put to death in the flesh but made alive by the Spirit."

Colossians 1:15–20 (Italics mine): "Jesus is the image of the invisible God, the firstborn of *all* creation. For by Him *all* things were created, *both* in the heavens and on earth, visible and invisible, whether thrones or dominions or rulers or authorities– *all* things have been created through Him and for Him. He is before *all* things, and in Him *all* things hold together. He is also head of the body, the church; and He is the beginning, the firstborn from the dead, so that He Himself will come to have first place in everything. For it was the *Father's* good pleasure for all the fullness to dwell in Him, and through Him to reconcile *all* things to Himself, having made peace through the blood of His cross; through Him, *I say*, whether things on earth or things in heaven."

All Really Means All

Jesus's finished work included all people … everyone!

John 12:32 (Italics mine): "And I, if I am lifted up from the earth, will draw *all* to Myself."

Romans 4:24 says, "All have been justified freely by His grace through the redemption that is in Christ Jesus."

Romans 6:10 (Italics mine): "For *the death* that He died, He died to sin once for *all*; but *the life* that He lives, He lives to God."

1 Timothy 4:9–10 (Italics mine): "This *is* a faithful saying and worthy of all acceptance. For to this *end* we both labor and suffer reproach, because we trust in the living God, who is *the* Savior of *all* men, especially of those who believe."

Romans 11:36 (Italics mine): "For of Him and through Him and to Him *are all* things, to whom *be* glory forever."

Hebrews 1:3 (Italics mine): "Jesus, being the brightness of *His* glory and the express image of His person, and upholding *all* things by the word of His power, when He had by Himself purged our sins, sat down at the right hand of the Majesty on high."

Hebrews 7:27 (Italics mine): "Jesus does not need to daily, as those high priests, to offer up sacrifices, first for His own sins and then for the people's, for this He did once for *all* when He offered up Himself."

Hebrews 8:11 (Italics mine): "None of them shall teach his neighbor, and none his brother, saying, 'Know the LORD,' for *all* shall know Me, from the least of them to the greatest of them."

Hebrews 9:12 (Italics mine): "Not with the blood of goats and calves, but with His own blood He entered the Most Holy Place once *for all*, having obtained eternal redemption."

Hebrews 10:10 (Italics mine): "By that will we have been sanctified through the offering of the body of Jesus Christ once *for all*."

In Christ Before Creation

'Gospel' means Good News! The Good News of the New Covenant of the Grace of Jesus Christ is NOT a potential gospel (i.e., "*If* you ask Jesus to forgive your sins, He will and He will come into your life"). NO! It is a historical fact ... an objective truth. He has done it all for you already. Now for you to benefit from what He has done for you, you believe what He has already done and receive what He's already given you!

Gold doesn't become gold when you discover it. It was always gold right where it was. Christ doesn't come into you when you ask Him and believe that He will. No! He has always been there. You were placed in Christ before creation, and that manifested itself in time and space at Jesus's Finished Work at the Cross.

Ephesians 1:4 (MIRROR): "God associated us in Christ before the fall of the world! Jesus is God's mind made up about us! He always knew in His love that He would present us again face-to-face before Him in blameless innocence. (The implications of the fall are completely cancelled. God found us in Christ before he lost us in Adam!)"

2 Corinthians 5:14–21 says, "The love of Christ resonates within us and leaves us with only one conclusion: Jesus died humanity's death; therefore, in God's logic every individual simultaneously died. Now if all were included in His death, they were equally included in His resurrection. This unveiling of His love redefines human life! Whatever reference we could have of ourselves outside of our association with Christ is no longer relevant.

"Now, in the light of your co-inclusion in His death and resurrection, whoever you thought you were before, in Christ you are a brand-new person! The old ways of seeing yourself and everyone else are over. Acquaint yourself with the new!

God the Father was in Christ Jesus reconciling the world (cosmos) to Himself, not counting their sins or trespasses against them!

"God's act of reconciliation is the mandate of our ministry. Our ministry declares the finished work of Jesus for ALL people! God has placed this message in us. He now announces His friendship with every individual from within us! The voice God has in Christ He now has in us; we are God's ambassadors. Our lives exhibit the urgency of God to persuade everyone to realize the reconciliation of their redeemed identity.

"This is the divine exchange! Jesus, who knew no sin, became our sin and gave us His righteousness ... His right standing with God became ours at that moment!"

A Completed Victory

Santo Calarco wrote, "The purpose of preaching the Gospel is to inform the world that it is finished and so enter into it and enjoy it! The Greek word for gospel (evangelion) literally means finished work! The English word evangelism comes from the Greek word (evangelizomia) for gospel and simply means the proclamation and declaration of a finished work! It is finished!"

This word was used in the ancient Greek world to announce a completed victory! The work of Jesus is not finished when we respond! When we hear about the finished work, we do respond and enter into and enjoy that which is already finished!

The finished work includes God's mercy. Many of us used to believe that mercy was connected to God withholding punishment for breaking His laws and instead He punished Jesus. We believed that we sin, we break a law, we deserve to be punished but because of the death of Jesus, God punished Jesus instead of us and withholds punishment from us, which is mercy. However, those beliefs were incorrect!

We saw mercy in terms of *withholding punishment* for sin which we defined as bad behavior, or breaking the law! However, Psalm 41:4 says, "Have mercy on me, Lord; *heal me,* for I have sinned against you." This verse shows that sin requires healing, not punishment! Mercy is set in parallel to healing, not withholding and transferring punishment! Sin requires healing because it is a sickness: bad behavior is the result of the sin-sickness. Mercy is not withholding punishment; rather, mercy is administering healing!

Since sin is sickness, then the cross is about healing!

1 Peter 2:24 says, "He himself bore our sins in His body at the cross, that we might die to sin and live to righteousness. By His wounds you have been HEALED! Sin is sickness and the cross was mercy and healing ... not withholding punishment!"

It's Done and It Lasts Forever

Jesus did what the Father sent Him to do, then He finished everything! He ended it all!

In John 19:28 and 30, Jesus's words, "It is finished," appear at the cross—thus we get the phrase: "Jesus's finished work at the cross."

John 19:28–30 (Parenthesis mine): "After this, Jesus, knowing that all was now finished, said (to fulfill the Scripture), 'I thirst.' A jar full of sour wine stood there, so they put a sponge full of the sour wine on a hyssop branch and held it to His mouth. When Jesus had received the sour wine, He said, 'It is finished,' and He bowed His head and gave up His spirit."

"It is finished," one of Jesus's most important statements, is translated from the single Greek word *tetelestai*. The grammatical structure of the Greek word, *perfect passive indicative*, is very important.

The perfect tense indicates that the *progress of an action has been completed and the result of that action is ongoing and with full effect*. The passive voice indicates that the subject of the *sentence is being acted upon*, and the indicative mood indicates *a statement of fact* or an actual occurrence from the writer's or speaker's perspective.

Jesus began everything, and He finished everything. The New Testament was originally written in Greek, and the first letter of the Greek alphabet, the beginning, is alpha. The last, the end, is omega.

Revelation 21:6 says, "And He also said, 'It is finished! I am the Alpha and the Omega– the Beginning and the End. To all who are thirsty I will give freely (without cost) from the springs of the water of life.'"

Revelation 22:13 says, "I am the Alpha and the Omega, the First and the Last, the Beginning and the End."

It Was All His Doing

The Father, Jesus, and the Holy Spirit finished everything us! Many of us have believed the lie that we did something to help Jesus finish His work! We've been taught by well-meaning, but misguided, religious people that we must do our part ('transactional salvation').

This teaching has many versions, but it basically says that we are separated from God because of our sin and that we must: confess (list out) our sins; sincerely repent (their definition is to be genuinely remorseful about both your actions and your being born totally depraved), ask for God's forgiveness, ask Jesus to come in to your heart; make Him the Lord of your life; and then prove that all of the above was genuine by changing your actions and behavior to conform with that particular denomination or organization's view of right and wrong. That's all performance-based effort on our part and ignores God's grace and Jesus's finished work at the cross. In essence, this view makes US our own savior because of what *we do*.

In contrast, scripture tells us that it's all God's doing! That's really good news!

1 Corinthians 1:30 (MIRROR) (Italics mine): "*Of God's doing are we in Christ.* He is both the genesis and genius of our wisdom; a wisdom that reveals how righteous, sanctified and redeemed we already are in Him."

2 Corinthians 5:18-9: "Now all things *are* of God, who has reconciled us to Himself through Jesus Christ, and has given us the ministry of reconciliation, that is, that God was in Christ reconciling the world to Himself, not imputing their trespasses or sins to them, and has committed to us the word of reconciliation."

1 Corinthians 2:12 (MIRROR): "The Spirit proceeding from God unveils the gifts of His generosity. He has graced us with understanding so that we may know what He has always had in mind for us; this is so unlike the secular spirit of the wisdom of the world where everything has a price tag!"

Christ is the unveiling of the mystery of God's wisdom: now

know how God redeemed our righteousness and our wholeness in Christ. In God's economy, Christ represents us; what mankind could never achieve through personal discipline and willpower as taught in every religion, God's faith accomplished in Christ. Of His desire are we in Christ; we are associated in oneness with Him. Our wisdom is sourced in this union! Also, our righteousness and holiness originate from Him!

Holiness equals wholeness and harmony of someone's spirit, soul, and body. Our redemption is sanctioned in Him. He redeemed our identity, our sanity, our health, our joy, our peace, our innocence, and our complete well-being!

What Jesus Accomplished
In His Finished Work At The Cross

Look at some of what Jesus accomplished in His Finished Work at the cross …

He justified you! The Greek word 'dikaioo' is translated as justified. It means to render righteous or such he ought to be; to show, exhibit, evince, one to be righteous, such as he is and wishes himself to be considered; to declare, pronounce, one to be just, righteous, or such as he ought to be.

Romans 3:24 says, "Being *justified* freely by His grace through the redemption that is in Christ Jesus."

Even though mankind thought we were not right with God and were 'enemies in our minds (but never objectively),' God did what was right: He made us right with Him. He did that freely at the cross, without our asking or deserving it!

Colossians 1:21–22 says, "And you, who once were alienated and enemies in your mind by wicked works, yet now He has reconciled in the body of His flesh through death, to present you holy, and blameless and above reproach in His sight."

He purified you! The Greek word 'katahros' is translated as purified. It means clean, pure; purified by fire; in a similitude, like a vine cleansed by pruning and so fitted to bear fruit.

John 15:3 says, "You have already been pruned and purified by the message I have given you."

1 Corinthians 1:30 (NLT): "God has united you with Christ Jesus. For our benefit God made Him to be wisdom itself. Christ made us right with God; He made us pure and holy, and He freed us from sin."

1 Thessalonians 5:23 (AMP): "Now may the God of peace Himself sanctify you through and through [that is, separate you from profane and vulgar things, make you pure and whole and undamaged— consecrated to Him —set apart for His purpose]; and may your spirit and soul and body be kept complete and [be found] blameless at the coming of our Lord Jesus Christ. Faithful and absolutely trustworthy is He who is calling you [to Himself

for your salvation], and He will do it [He will fulfill His call by making you holy, guarding you, watching over you, and protecting you as His own]."

Acts 15:9–10 says, "And God, who knows the heart, testified to them giving them the Holy Spirit, just as He also did to us; and He made no distinction between us and them, cleansing their hearts by faith."

Hebrews 9:14 (MOUNCE): "… how much more will the blood of Christ, who through the eternal Spirit offered himself without blemish to God, purify our conscience from dead works to worship the living God!"

He Glorified You And Sanctified You

God glorified you! The Greek word 'doxoso' is translated as glorified. It means to think, suppose, be of opinion, to praise, extol, magnify, celebrate, to honor, do honor to, hold in honor, to make glorious, adorn with luster, clothe with splendor, to impart glory to something, render it excellent, to make renowned, render illustrious, to cause the dignity and worth of some person or thing to become manifest and acknowledged.

Jesus did all that for YOU at the cross!

Romans 8:30 says, "Moreover whom He predestined, these He also called; whom He called, these He also justified; and whom He justified, these He also glorified."

Colossians 1:27 says, "Christ in you, the hope of glory!"

God sanctified you! The Greek word 'hagiazo' is translated as sanctified. It means to render or acknowledge, or to be venerable, to separate from profane things and dedicate to God, consecrate things to God, dedicate people to God, to purify, to cleanse externally, to purify by expiation: free from the guilt of sin, to purify internally by renewing of the soul.

1 Corinthians 6:11 says, "And such were some of you. But you were washed, but you were sanctified, but you were justified in the name of the Lord Jesus and by the Spirit of our God."

Galatians 3:26 (AMP): "For you have been reborn from above— spiritually transformed, renewed, sanctified and are all children of God [set apart for His purpose with full rights and privileges] through faith in Christ Jesus."

Colossians 3:12 (AMP): "So, as God's own chosen people, who are holy [set apart, sanctified for His purpose] and well-beloved [by God Himself], put on a heart of compassion, kindness, humility, gentleness, and patience [which has the power to endure whatever injustice or unpleasantness comes, with good temper]."

Hebrews 10:10 (AMP): "And in accordance with the will of God we have been sanctified [that is, set apart as holy for God and His purposes] through the offering of the body of Jesus Christ (the Messiah, the Anointed) once for all."

Jesus Reconciled You, Redeemed You and Made You Friends With God

Jesus made us friends with God!

John 15:3 says, "Greater love has no one than this, than to lay down one's life for his friends."

John 15:15 says, "No longer do I call you servants, for a servant does not know what his master is doing; but I have called you friends, for all things that I heard from My Father I have made known to you."

He redeemed you! The Greek word 'exagorazo' is translated as redeemed. It means to redeem by payment of a price, to recover from the power of another, to ransom, buy off, metaphor of Christ freeing mankind from the dominion of the Mosaic Law at the price of his vicarious death.

Galatians 3:13–14 says, "Christ has redeemed us from the curse of the law, having become a curse for us (for it is written, 'Cursed is everyone who hangs on a tree'), He redeemed us in order that the blessing given to Abraham might come to the Gentiles through Christ Jesus, so that by faith we might receive the promise of the Spirit."

1 Corinthians 8:6 says, "For us there is but one God, the Father, who is the source of all things, and we *exist* for Him; and one Lord, Jesus Christ, by whom are all things that have been created, and we exist and have life and have been redeemed through Him."

God reconciled you! The Greek word 'Katallasso' is translated as reconciled. It means to change, exchange, as coins for others of equivalent value, to reconcile (those who are at variance), return to favor with, be reconciled to one, to receive one into favor.

Romans 5:10 says, "For if when we were enemies we were reconciled to God through the death of His Son, much more, having been reconciled, we shall be saved by His life."

2 Corinthians 5:18 says, "Now all things *are* of God, who has reconciled us to Himself through Jesus Christ, and has given us the ministry of reconciliation."

Ephesians 2:16 says, "Together as one body, Christ reconciled both groups to God by means of His death on the cross, and our hostility toward each other was put to death."

Colossians 1:20–22 says, "And through Him God reconciled everything to Himself. He made peace with everything in heaven and on earth by means of Christ's blood on the cross. And you, who once were alienated and enemies in your mind by wicked works, yet He has now reconciled you in His fleshly body through death, in order to present you before Him holy and blameless and beyond reproach."

Jesus Totally Took Care of Your Sin Problem And Made You Right With God!

God took all your sins away and forgave them all (past, present, and future!)

Colossians 2:13 (NLT): "You were dead because of your sins and because your sinful nature was not yet cut away. Then God made you alive with Christ, for He forgave all our sins."

(MIRROR): "You were once spiritually dead, as confirmed in your constant failure; being bound to a lifestyle ruled by the distorted desires of the flesh, but now God has made you alive together with Him, having forgiven you all your trespasses."

God made you righteous! 2 Corinthians 5:21 tells us that Jesus became our sin and gave us His righteousness. We call that *The Great Exchange.*

God chose you before creation and created a new you!

Ephesians 1:4 (GNT): "Even before the world was made, God had already chosen us to be His through our union with Christ, so that we would be holy and without fault before him."

2 Corinthians 5:17 (MIRROR): "Now in the light of your co-inclusion in His death and resurrection, whoever you thought you were before, In Christ you are a brand-new person! The old ways of seeing yourself and everyone else are over. Acquaint yourself with the new!"

Many translations say, "If anyone is in Christ, he is a new creation." Mirror footnotes: "The 'if' is not a condition, it is the conclusion of the revelation of the gospel! Mankind is in Christ by God's doing. For so long we studied this verse on its own and interpreted the 'if' as a condition! Paul did not say, 'If anyone is in Christ,' he said 'THEREFORE if anyone is in Christ …' The 'therefore' immediately includes verses 14 to 16! If God's faith sees everyone in Christ in His death, then they were certainly also in Christ in his resurrection! Jesus did not reveal a 'potential' you, He revealed the truth about you so that you may know the truth about yourself and be free indeed!"

He Set You Free from The Law, Made You His Child, Chose To Live In You And Never Condemns You

God relates to you totally without condemnation!

Romans 8:1 says, "There is therefore now no condemnation for those who are in Christ Jesus."

(MIRROR): "Now the decisive conclusion is this: in Christ, every bit of condemning evidence against us is cancelled! (The 'in Christ' revelation is key to God's dealing with mankind. It is the PIN-code of the Bible.)"

God set you free from the law of sin and death!

Romans 8:2 says, "The law of the life-giving Spirit in Christ Jesus has set you free from the law of sin and death."

God made you a child of Theirs and fellow heir with Christ!

Romans 8:17 says, "And since we are His children, we are His heirs. In fact, together with Christ we are heirs of God's glory. But if we are to share His glory, we must also share His suffering."

Galatians 4:7 says, "So you are no longer a slave but a son, and if you are a son, then you are also an heir through God."

God made your body the temple of the Holy Spirit!

1 Corinthians 6:19 says, "Do you not know that you are God's temple and that God's Spirit lives in you?"

God joined you to Them and made you one spirit with Them!

1 Corinthians 6:17 (MIRROR): "In our union with Him we are one spirit with the Lord."

God always leads you in the triumph and knowledge of Christ!

2 Corinthians 2:14 says, "But thanks be to God who always leads us in triumphal procession in Christ and who makes known through us the fragrance that consists of the knowledge of Him in every place."

God made you one with everyone!

Galatians 3:28 says, "There is neither Jew nor Greek, there is neither slave nor free, there is neither male nor female--for all of you are one in Christ Jesus."

God Set You Free And Made You Alive In Christ! He Has Blessed You

God set you free!

Galatians 5:1 says, "For freedom Christ has set us free."

(MIRROR): "Christ defines your faith; He is your freedom from anything from which the law could never free you! Find your firm footing in this freedom. Do not let religion trip you up again and harness you to a system of rules and obligations!"

God made you alive with Christ!

Ephesians 2:4–5 says, "But God, being rich in mercy, because of His great love with which He loved us, even though we were dead in transgressions, made us alive together with Christ- by grace you are saved!"

God already blessed you with every spiritual blessing in the Heavenly places!

Ephesians 1:3 says, "Blessed is the God and Father of our Lord Jesus Christ, who has blessed us with every spiritual blessing in the heavenly realms in Christ."

God redeemed you by Their grace!

Ephesians 1:7 says, "In Him we have redemption through His blood, the forgiveness of our trespasses, according to the riches of His grace."

It was God's will before creation to make you Their own possession!

Ephesians 1:11 says, "In Christ we too have been claimed as God's own possession, since we were predestined according to the one purpose of him who accomplishes all things according to the counsel of His will."

God saved you!

Ephesians 2:8 (MIRROR): "Your salvation is not a reward for good behavior! It was a grace thing from start to finish; you had no hand in it. Even the gift to believe simply reflects His faith! (By grace you are! Saved by the gift of faith; grace reveals who we are and the faith of God persuades us of it! You did not invent faith; it was God's faith to begin with! It is from faith to faith, (Romans 1:17) He is both the source and conclusion of faith. (Hebrews 12:2)"

He Seated You In Heaven and Gave You Boldness and Confidence. He Made You Complete

God sealed you with the promise of His spirit!

Ephesians 1:13 says, "In Him, you also, after listening to the message of truth, the gospel of your salvation—having also believed, you were sealed in Him with the Holy Spirit of promise."

God seated you in Heaven with Them already!

Ephesians 2:6 says, "… And He raised us up with Him and seated us with Him in the heavenly realms in Christ Jesus …"

God made you a citizen of Heaven!

Philippians 3:20 says, "Our citizenship is in heaven …"

God gave you boldness and confident access to Them through Christ's faith!

Ephesians 3:12 says "… In whom we have boldness and confident access to God because of Christ's faithfulness."

God took you out of darkness and put you in the light of Christ!

Ephesians 5:8 says, "You were formerly in darkness, but now you are Light in the Lord."

Colossians 1:13 (MIRROR): "He rescued us from the dominion of darkness (the sense-ruled world, dominated by the law of performance) and relocated us into the kingdom where the love of His son rules! (Darkness is not a force, it is the absence of light. A darkened understanding veiled the truth of our redeemed design from us. What *empowered* darkness was the lie that we believed about ourselves!)"

God made you complete!

Colossians 2:10 (NLT): "So you also are complete through your union with Christ, who is the head over every ruler and authority."

Christ is your life, and God will reveal you with Him in glory!

Colossians 3:4 says, "When Christ (who is your life) appears, then you too will be revealed in glory with Him."

God Accepted You, Gave You Peace and Continues To Reveal His Grace To You Every Day

Here's the last of my list of what Jesus accomplished in His Finished Work at the cross for us ... but my list only touches the surface of everything Jesus did!

God gave you peace to guard your heart and mind!

Philippians 4:7 says, "The peace of God that surpasses all understanding will guard your hearts and minds in Christ Jesus."

God supplies all your needs!

Philippians 4:19 says, "My God will supply your every need according to his glorious riches in Christ Jesus."

God accepted you!

Romans 15:7 says, "Therefore, accept one another, just as Christ also accepted us to the glory of God."

God will reveal more and more of Their grace to you every day!

Ephesians 2:5–7 (Italics mine): "By grace you have been saved and God raised *us* up together, and made *us* sit together in the heavenly *places* in Christ Jesus, that in the ages to come He might show the exceeding riches of His grace in *His* kindness toward us in Christ Jesus."

CHAPTER 6
ONENESS, UNION, AND IDENTITY

The Unseen vs. The Seen Realm

Jesus often refers to the 'Kingdom of God' or the 'Kingdom of Heaven.' Most often He uses parables or stories that have a deeper meaning than what's on the surface. In every case, He's helping us see something that we can't see or perceive through our five senses … *what appears to be true* in the world around us.

The Apostle Paul refers to the *unseen eternal spiritual realm* as opposed to the *seen and temporal* realm of the world.

The following three versions of the same passage are key to *seeing what really is.*

2 Corinthians 4:16–18 (MSG) (Italics mine): "So we're not giving up. How could we! Even though on the outside it often looks like things are falling apart on us, on the inside, where God is making new life, not a day goes by without His unfolding grace. These hard times are small potatoes compared to the coming good times, the lavish celebration prepared for us. There's *far more here than meets the eye.* The things we see now are here today, gone tomorrow. But *the things we can't see now* will last forever."

2 Corinthians 4:18 (NIV) (Italics mine): "So we fix our eyes not on what is seen, but on what is unseen, since *what is seen is temporary, but what is unseen is eternal.*"

2 Corinthians 4:18 (MIRROR): "We are not keeping any score of what seems so obvious to the senses on the surface; it is fleeting and irrelevant; it is the *unseen eternal realm within us* which has our full attention and captivates our gaze!"

Don Keathley, Pastor of Grace Point Community Church in Houston, Texas, often posts great Facebook posts about grace. He says, "A REVELATION of grace, the finished work of the cross and an understanding of your true identity has prepared you to be on the transition team that will learn to move the total supply *from the invisible kingdom within* to a *visible manifestation* that will *meet every need you have.*"

Another quote from Pastor Don Keathley: "IF YOU ARE AFRAID to read and explore outside your indoctrinated comfort zone with an open heart under the direction of the Spirit of Truth, it is a good indication that religion has done its work in your life.

When you get outside your religious paradigm you might not only discover deeper truth but also enjoy the driving out of that fear as perfect love does its work in your life ..."

From *Patmos* by Baxter Kruger: "Faith is seeing with Jesus's eyes, seeing what is. From faith to faith, the Word believes."

The Great Darkness

The primary reason many of us are unable to *see what really is* is that we have believed lies about ourselves, God, and others. We have believed what our five senses appear to teach us is true, and we have believed what human teachers (well-meaning but misguided) have taught us that *seems* to be right.

We have been taught (and we believed) the worst lie of all history—the lie that Adam and Eve believed as a result of their disobeying God, *the lie of separation.*

The *lie of separation* and our *assumption that it is real* IS the *Great Darkness*! The *lie of separation* says that because of our sin, God separated Himself from us, is angry with us, has to be appeased, can't stand to be in our presence, and that we are eternally doomed to be punished in God's uniquely designed torture chamber unless we gain and maintain God's favor by something(s) we do. This whole concept is flawed and is a lie.

God never separated Himself from Adam and Eve! He pursued them, came to them, loved them and protected them. He has never separated Himself from us! The only separation has been in our minds. It's subjectively true to us because it feels true, but objectively, it's not true!

The only place the Bible talks about this separation is Isaiah 59. The chapter starts out by saying that God is surely able to save us. Then it says, "Your sins have separated you from your God." It concludes with: "God's own arm has saved you and given you His righteousness!" Colossians 1:20–21 tells us that God already reconciled us all to Him (NOT vice versa) and that was because we were 'enemies in our minds.'

Believing this heinous *lie of separation* has put mankind in the *great darkness* where we have been unable to *see what really is.*

Fortunately, there's Good News! Colossians 1:12–15 says, "We give thanks to the Father who has qualified *us* to be partakers of the inheritance of the saints in the light. He has delivered us from the power of darkness and conveyed us into the kingdom of the Son of His love, in whom we have redemption through His blood, the forgiveness of sins."

God put us in the light! He delivered us from the power of darkness and put us in the kingdom of Jesus, where the truth, What Really Is, is that we are reconciled, redeemed and forgiven!

Objectively, we are totally right and one with God. That's the basis for our true identity. It doesn't always look like that in the seen world, but in the unseen world, the truth of all eternity exists. Everything changes for the better when we start to see and believe *what really is*!

The Teacher Will Show You!

How do we *see what really is* in the unseen world? We have the Holy Spirit of Jesus, living in us, who is constantly revealing the truth to us! The Teacher teaches us what really is!

Hebrews 2:9 (MIRROR): "Let us then consider Him (Jesus) in such a way that we may clearly perceive what God is saying to mankind in Him."

Matthews 23:10 says, "And do not be called teachers; for One is your Teacher, the Christ."

Luke 12:12 says, "For the Holy Spirit will teach you in that very hour what you ought to say."

John 14:26 says, "But the Helper, the Holy Spirit, whom the Father will send in My name, He will teach you all things, and bring to your remembrance all things that I said to you."

Hebrews 8:11 says, "None of them shall teach his neighbor, and none his brother, saying, 'Know the LORD,' for all shall know Me, from the least of them to the greatest of them."

1 John 2:27 says, "But the anointing which you have received from Him abides in you, and you do not need that anyone teach you ..."

1 Corinthians 2:13 says, "... the Holy Spirit teaches, comparing spiritual things with spiritual."

The Teacher sees us differently than we see ourselves. To *see what really is*, what is eternal, we need to listen to The Teacher and thus learn how God sees us and believe God instead of what we believe about ourselves from the world and what religious people have told us!

Baxter Kruger said during a seminar in Lawrence, Ks, that the issue is union or separation. We tend to either see our humanity as separated from the Lord ... or as a living union (abide). We see 'secular' and 'spiritual.' But, there is no secular, only the evil one's perversion. There really is no secular world at all. Jesus has filled the whole creation with Himself!

Baxter refers to the evil one as 'Ophis,' which is the Greek word for 'serpent or snake' used in the New Testament. I like to use 'Ophis' because it sounds like (and reminds me of our word) Doofus! ('Doofus'—someone who hasn't got a clue! –Urban Dictionary.)

The Perceived Darkness of Separation

One of the key areas where we need to *see what really is* is in regard to sin.

What is true in the unseen spiritual realm, the Kingdom of God, includes:

- That Jesus took ALL your (and everyone's) sin away!
- That God forgave ALL your (and everyone's) sin!
- That God keeps no list of anyone's sin!
- That God chooses not to remember anyone's sin!
- That God doesn't hold anyone's sin against them!
- That God doesn't bring anyone's sin up to them!
- That Sin is not an issue between God and us!

When those who have been involved in religion and who have believed the *great lie* that results in the perceived *great darkness of separation* hear the above, they almost immediately ask, "But what about 1 John 1:9?" A representative traditional translation is:

1 John 1:9 (KJV): "*If* we confess our sins, He is faithful and just to forgive us *our* sins and to cleanse us from all unrighteousness."

A thorough study reveals that 'if' is a declaration and could better be translated as 'since.' 'Confess' means to agree with. The Mirror Translation helps us as follows:

1 John 1:9 (MIRROR): "When we communicate what God says about our sins, we discover what He believes concerning our redeemed oneness and innocence! We are cleansed from every distortion we believed about ourselves! Likeness is redeemed! (The word traditionally translated as "confession" is the word homologeo, from home, the same, and logeo, to speak. In the context of verse 7, this suggests that we say what God says about us!)."

Seeing what really is reminds us that God sees that ALL our sins have already been taken care of. He redeemed us and made us innocent! When we start to believe what God believes to be true objectively in the unseen, eternal realm, then what *appears* to be true in the seen but temporary world can be dismissed accordingly!

Pastor Don Keathley said, "WHEN IT FINALLY DAWNS on the church that sin is a disease to be healed not a wrong to be punished the church will finally put to rest a lot of wrong notions on how the Father deals with sin. Then judging and knowing others after the flesh will cease, and the love by which the world will know we are followers of Jesus will cover the earth... It is already breaking out in places and will continue to surge by leaps and bounds."

Four Circles

Following are some comments (paraphrased) from Baxter Kruger during a seminar in Lawrence, Kansas:

Adam and Eve's deception literally left them in the dark … blind to what was true. Even though Jesus fully did away with Adam's race in His finished work at the cross, and even though He made us all objectively right with God forever, we still aren't individually able to see that because our minds are still in the dark.

I've found that it's very helpful to see what we tend to do when we can't *see what really is*.

We tend to create something we can see … in our imagination, and then we defend it with a vengeance because it's all we think we have! That's why so many well-meaning, but deceived, people get very angry when they hear about pure grace and hear that sin is no longer an issue for anyone in their relationship with God!

Well-meaning people are determined, but they are blind. They cannot *see what is*, so they invent things that they can see in their own head, and they die of exhaustion pursuing their invented ways of 'getting in' with God. If we believe that we are separated from the Lord (and we are not), then we must find a way back. One's eternal existence would hang in the balance. That makes us wide open to anyone's claim to know how to get back to God.

But since we are NOT separated, to begin with, *any idea as to how to get back to God won't work! And we eventually die of exhaustion or sadness or cynicism or despair … even though we have been faithful and true to 'the' cause! Wrong ideas lead to destruction!*

The battle is between believing and seeing Union or Separation. Separation *appears* to be true because of what we can see, hear, feel, taste and touch with our five senses. But what is real and eternal is Union/Oneness!

John 16:20 (MIRROR) (Jesus): "In that day you will know

that just as I am in my Father, you are in me and I am in you!"

Picture 4 circles, with one fitting into the other. The outer circle is the Father, then Jesus in the Father, then us in Jesus, and the Spirit in us! This spells inseparable, intimate oneness! Note that it is not our *knowing this* that positions Jesus in the Father or us in them! Our knowing simply awakens us to the reality of our redeemed union! Gold does not become gold when it is discovered, but it certainly becomes currency!

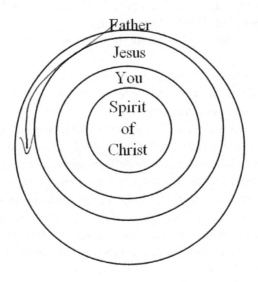

Radiate Life

Paraphrased thoughts from Baxter Kruger (from a seminar in Lawrence, Kansas):

As humans, in our own power, we are incapable of helping anyone see the truth about *what really is*. The Holy Spirit of Christ must reveal it to people. We, of course, want everyone to know the truth, and we tell them, but we don't have the power to get them out of the darkness and convince them. Jesus said:

John 8:12 (MIRROR): "I am the light of the world— whoever journeys with Me shall not walk in darkness, but will radiate the light of life!"

The moment you meet (discover) Christ in you, you experience His *life*, His hope, His freedom, His joy in the midst of the darkness! You realize you are free!

When we believe the *lie of separation* that keeps us in *the great darkness*, then we think WE have to find our way to God. The Greeks (and Calvinists) tried to do it through their mind and the Jews (legalists) and the Roman Church—through the law. Others (Western Evangelicals) try through a combination of the two. The law became our default setting on how to get back to God.

As long as a person has made an agreement with Diabolos that God's love is conditional, limited and exclusive, that person won't be able to *see or hear* love and grace and Finished Work and inclusion until they break that agreement!

Our writing and teaching must not be with the intent to inform or explain or convince; rather, they should be with the goal of giving *people eyes to encounter Jesus!* Eyes to *see what really is!* Our teaching won't really say what we want until something else happens ... until the Holy Spirit transforms our words into an encounter with Jesus Himself!

C.S. Lewis said, "We can be in full possession of all the facts and yet miss their meaning."

George MacDonald said, "Good souls many will one day be horrified at the things they now believe of God."

Jesus Means That God And Humanity Are Together!

Thoughts from Baxter Kruger's seminar in Lawrence, Kansas (paraphrased):

The point of John's gospel is that Jesus was face to face with His Father before creation, and *all things* came into being through Him. He became flesh to meet us in our great darkness and death so that He could be in us, inside our darkness, and we could see with His eyes! We must see *all things in Christ*. Today John would say, "How could anyone use my gospel to teach that God does not love the whole world? The Father found us all, Jews and Gentiles, even the Romans, *in Jesus!*"

Jesus *is* the eternal message of God to us!

T.F. Torrence said, "Not God alone, but God and humanity together, constitute the meaning of the Word of God."

John The Apostle would say, "Not God alone, but God and humanity together, constitute the meaning of JESUS!"

Jesus means that God and humanity are together forever!

The opposite of together is separated.

Jesus means that God and humanity are not separated but together in union! And this union is the word of God! It's what God is saying to us all!

Pastor Don Keathley said, "'For God has consigned all men to disobedience that He may have mercy on them all.' Romans 11:32 ... Doesn't that just kick the bee-jabbers out of your theology?"

Check Your Filter

In one of his daily video posts, Steve McVey reminds us of the Old Testament story where Elisha and his servant were surrounded by a huge army of enemies who intended to kill them (subjective truth). The servant couldn't *see what really is,* (objective truth) so Elisha asked God to "open his eyes." When God did, the servant saw (objective truth) that God's army was much bigger than the enemy and there was no problem at all!

Steve points out that happiness comes from happenings. It comes and goes with circumstances and situations. It's subjective. However, God's joy is objective! It comes from what's eternal and real but unseen!

God wants to enable us to *see what really is* by using His filter.

"Everybody has a filter which he takes about with him, through which, from the indefinite mass of acts, he gathers in those suited to confirm his prejudices. Rare, very rare, are those who check their filter." –Henri du Lubac; *Paradoxes of Faith.*

Baxter Kruger says in *Jesus and The Undoing of Adam:* "For our ideas and concepts, our categories, assumptions and notions, function together as a pair of glasses, as it were, through which we perceive and make sense of our world. Without mental glasses of some sort we would be blind and have no way of conceiving the realities pressing upon us or of processing the endless variety of information coming to us. It would be like trying to dance with someone in pitch-black dark to the music of three or four different songs at the same time. The fact that we all have mental glasses – and inevitably use them – is not where the problem lies. The difficulty lies in the fact that we have the wrong prescription. That is to say, that our ideas and concepts, our categories and assumptions, are skewed."

Steve McVey said, "Today … and every day, we can pray: Holy Spirit, 'Show me lies I've believed and show me the truth.'"

Two Radically Different Ways of Living

Seeing life through the lens of union or the lens of separation will produce two radically different ways of living. The assumption of separation produces *the great darkness* which then makes us see everything through the lens of Separation. Jesus's light *exposes the great darkness* and reveals His Truth, then we see through His lens of union.

When you live in *the great darkness,* you can't see what is real and true. You can't *see what really is.* You can't hear God clearly. You're susceptible to more lies from the evil one. You never really experience true peace and joy.

In *the great darkness,* you believe the lie that you are not in God's good graces; you believe the lie that you are not in right standing with Him. As a result, you create something you can *see* in your imagination, some *way* to view God and some *way* to get back into relationship with Him and back in His good graces.

Most likely you adopt some *way* that someone else, maybe your parents or some denomination or teacher (who has a title and letters after their name), believes. Then you adopt that *way* as your own, never question it, and you then defend it with a vengeance … because it's all you have. We see life through the lens of separation.

However, The Spirit of Christ in us (union) continually reveals Christ's light and life to us!

1 Corinthians 13:12–13 (Parenthesis mine): "For now we see in a mirror (subjectively) dimly, but then face to face (objectively). Now I know in part (subjectively), but then I shall know just as I also am known (objectively). And now abide faith, hope, love, these three; but the greatest of these *is* love."

Colossians 1:26–27 says, "This is the mystery which has been hidden from ages and from generations, but now has been revealed to His saints. To them God willed to make known what are the riches of the glory of this mystery among the Gentiles: which is Christ in you, the hope of glory."

Hebrews 11:1 (Italics mine): "Now faith is the assurance of

things hoped for, the conviction of things not seen."

Pastor Don Keathley said, "Grace has taught me that learning more and simply gathering more religious information does not bring any lasting transformation. Only a revelation of my true identity and communion with the Father brought what I longed for on a deep level in life."

Christ Is the Unveiling of God's Mystery

The following verses help us develop the correct lens (union with God) that we then use to *see what really is:*

1 Corinthians 2:12 (MIRROR): "The Spirit proceeding from God unveils the gifts of His generosity. He has graced us with understanding so that we may know what He has always had in mind for us; this is so unlike the secular spirit of the wisdom of the world where everything has a price tag!"

(Christ is the unveiling of the mystery of God's wisdom: now we know how God redeemed our righteousness and our wholeness in Christ. In God's economy, Christ represents us; what mankind could never achieve through personal discipline and willpower as taught in every religion, God's faith accomplished in Christ. Of His desire are we in Christ; we are associated in oneness with Him. Our wisdom is sourced in this union! Also, our righteousness and holiness originate from Him!

Holiness equals wholeness and harmony of someone's spirit, soul, and body. Our redemption is sanctioned in Him. He redeemed our identity, our sanity, our health, our joy, our peace, our innocence and our complete well-being!)

1 Corinthians 1:30 (MIRROR): Of God's doing are we in Christ. He is both the genesis and genius of our wisdom; a wisdom that reveals how righteous, sanctified and redeemed we already are in Him."

John 1:18 (MIRROR): "Until this moment God remained invisible to mankind; now the authentic begotten Son, the blueprint of mankind's design who represents the innermost being of God, the Son who is in the bosom of the Father, brings Him into full view! He is the official authority qualified to announce God! He is our guide who accurately declares and interprets the invisible God within us."

2 Corinthians 3:18 (MIRROR): "The days of window-shopping are over! In Christ every face is unveiled. In gazing with wonder at the blueprint likeness of God displayed in human form, we suddenly realize that we are looking at ourselves! Every

feature of His image is mirrored in us! This is the most radical transformation engineered by the Spirit of the Lord; we are led from an inferior mind-set to the revealed endorsement of our authentic identity."

Hebrews 11:1 (MIRROR): "Persuasion confirms confident expectation and proves the unseen world to be more real than the seen. Faith celebrates as certain what hope visualizes as future. (The shadow no longer substitutes the substance. Jesus is the substance of things hoped for, the evidence of everything the prophets foretold. The unveiling of Christ in human life completes mankind's every expectation. Colossians 1:27)"

The Nourishment of The Mature

Hebrews 5:14 (MIRROR): "This is the nourishment of the mature. They are those who have their faculties of perception trained as by gymnastic precision to distinguish the relevant from the irrelevant. (The mature are those who know the difference between the shadow and the substance; between the futility of the law of works and willpower to work righteousness, and righteousness revealed by the faith of God in THE FINISHED WORK OF CHRIST!)"

1 JOHN 4:16 (MIRROR): "We have come to know and believe the love that God has unveiled within us. God is love; love is who God is; to live in this place of conscious, constant love, is to live immersed in God and to feel perfectly at home in his indwelling. (You're not alone and adrift in the universe; you are at home in the Father's good pleasure!)"

Walking by faith (objective) and not by sight (subjective) is when you know that it is *finished* in all things for ALL people.

Pastor Don Keathley said, "Man's union with God was the Father's original thought that inspired creation. It was NEVER to be any other way, and guess what? It never has been any other way. You are one with your source of creation, never being without His image and likeness."

2 Timothy 1:9–10 (Italics mine): " *Jesus has saved us* and called *us* with a holy calling, not according to our works, but according to *His own purpose and grace which was given to us in Christ Jesus before time began,* but has now been revealed by the appearing of our Savior Jesus Christ, *who* has abolished death and brought life and immortality to light through the gospel."

1 Timothy 4:10 says, "For to this *end* we both labor and suffer reproach, because we trust in the living *God, who is the Savior of all men,* especially of those who believe."

Evil's Chief Trick

It can be very hard for religious people to give up favoring what they can see in the world dominated by our five senses and thus start *seeing what really is.*

Recently I gave a Mirror Bible to a dear friend of mine who is 'religious.' After reading the introduction, he commented, "It says that Christ accepted us, but I *know* that we have to accept Christ. I *know* there are things we have to do."

I asked, "How do you 'know' that?"

His reply was, "It's just obvious!"

This is evil one's CHIEF TRICK! He blinds us to how close the Lord really is—closer than the air we breathe. We are in Him, and He is in us, and He did that!

John 14:20 (Jesus) In that day you will know that I am in My Father, you are in me and I in you!

Jesus said in Matthew 11:28–30 (MSSG), "Are you tired? Worn out? Burned out on religion? Come to Me. Get away with Me and you'll recover your life. I'll show you how to take a real rest. Walk with Me and work with Me—watch how I do it. Learn the unforced rhythms of grace. I won't lay anything heavy or ill-fitting on you. Keep company with Me and you'll learn to live freely and lightly."

Jesus will give you rest from trying to 'get in' and will show you what is real ... in the unseen and eternal realm.

Pastor Don Keathley said, "Trying to achieve oneness with the Father is like trying to enter a room you are already in."

"I HAVE MINISTERED BOTH an exclusive gospel of 'them and us' and a gospel that is inclusive 'all included at the cross' and my honest evaluation is this. The inclusive gospel produces a more secure, holy living, loving, non-judgmental follower of Jesus than the 'us and them' turn or burn gospel I taught for over 35 years ever produced ... That is the simple truth from a Pastor of 47 years."

What Do You Do When You Can't See What Is?

Question: What do you do when you can't see what is?

Answer: You create something you can see ... in your imagination ... and then you defend it with a vengeance because it's all you think you have! The lie of separation from God is the chief of all lies. *Seeing what really is* is all about coming to behold Jesus in us!

Jesus said in John 8:12, "I am the light of the world; the one who follows Me shall not walk in the darkness, but shall have the light of LIFE!"

The moment you meet (discover) Christ in you, you experience His LIFE, His hope, His freedom, His joy in the midst of the darkness!

Many translations of John 1:14 state: "The Word became flesh and dwelt among us." However, a better translation would be 'in us' rather than 'among us.' Also, in Galatians 1:15–16, Paul states that when Christ appeared to him (as the Christ-hater, murdering 'Saul of the Pharisees'), God revealed Christ IN him and Christ IN (same word) the Gentiles! Christ is IN you, and He always has been! The same is true of everyone!

Francois DuToit said, "We often think that faith is to believe things we don't understand. No, blind faith is an illusion. The truth is: Faith SEES! Faith sees what is! The 'broken' me is the me that Jesus is in. He became 'sarx' (Greek: 'flesh'). He is with me in my darkness!

Jesus, who was in the beginning face-to-face with the Father, out of God's being, now is in us, in our darkness: THAT IS THE GOSPEL!"

Don Keathley: "If you feel safe and secure because you made a decision to accept Jesus then you don't understand the gospel. We are safe and secure because the Father through the Son in the Spirit made their decision to accept us before time began. See Ephesians 1:4 and then do your happy dance and trash your religious pride in what you did. Religion sees believing as something you must do to be saved. Grace sees believing as an effortless response to the revelation of what He has already done!"

Reality Is Union

What really is ... is *union*. We have been united with the Trinity! We live in oneness with them!

After 'the fall,' we read Genesis 3:8 (Italics mine): "And they *heard the voice* of the LORD *God* walking in the garden in the *cool of the day*: and Adam and his wife hid themselves from the presence of the LORD God amongst the trees of the garden."

'*God*' is translated from the Hebrew word 'Elohiym' which means 'Gods'—plural.

Cool is translated from the Hebrew word *ruwach*. Ruwach is the Hebrew word for the Spirit of God. Ruwach is found 378 times in the Old Testament and is only once (in Genesis 3:8) translated (incorrectly!) as 'cool.'

The text literally reads that they heard the Trinity (Father, Jesus) walking in The Spirit in the garden. The Trinity has always been a community, and They have included us in Their union!

It seems obvious that many of the Old Testament translators, when presented with the word Ruach, had no concept of the Trinity 'walking in the Spirit,' union, or our oneness with Them.

John 8:12 (Jesus): "Then Jesus spoke to them again, saying, 'I am the light of the world. He who follows Me shall not walk in darkness, but have the light of life.'"

In *Patmos*, Baxter Kruger writes, "Without an encounter with Jesus inside our own hearts, we have no liberation from Ophis' lies and no freedom to turn towards the Father. Indeed without the revelation of Jesus in us, we would never even know that we are in the dark at all! Jesus has no intention of being the Father's Son—the Anointed One—Lord of all creation ... without or apart from us! Christ in You, Jesus, the Living Word, the Great I Am—reveals Himself in all people and shares His eyes with us!"

Don Keathley: "For years when we heard something that conflicted with our traditional way of thinking or did not agree with our theology we immediately went to Scripture to validate its truth or error. I see today that the Holy Spirit that Jesus said would lead us into all truth is beginning to be the first place we take something new to, to test whether what we are hearing is true or not."

We Have Never Been Apart From God

The Holy Spirit of Christ lives in every person and has since Jesus's Finished Work at the Cross. The Spirit is like a 'tuning fork' that resonates inside us when The Spirit hears the proclamation that Christ is IN us, the hope of glory!

When you hear the truth of oneness/union, you will know it (unless your heart is stubbornly clinging to darkness) because you will sense the Holy Spirit of Christ in you resonating with the truth you hear!

However, when you hear the *lie of separation* taught, nothing resonates inside you. Instead, evil anger may fester in your darkened mind because it does not want to hear *union or oneness*. It only wants you to believe the *lie of separation*.

The assumption of separation is the great darkness.

Our relationship with God, our spiritual walk, hinges on whether we believe union … or separation. This belief will impact everything you think about yourself, God, and other people. The two are diametrically and diabolically opposed to each other.

As Baxter Kruger pleads, "Take sides with Jesus against Ophis' madness."

Law is the default setting from *religion* regarding how to *get back to God*. However, we have never been apart from God! Refuse to go there! Virtually all religion teaches some form of separation/law/works! Avoid religion like the plague it is!

There Is Only One Battle:
Union vs. Separation

Thoughts from Baxter Kruger's seminar in Lawrence, Kansas (paraphrased):

Seeing Papa with Jesus' eyes leads to life abounding. Without a revelation from Jesus, we would never know we're in the dark at all!

Don't live by applying Scripture to your life; rather, live from union with Papa! Jesus is in you, and He believes!

Take sides with Jesus against the way we *see* and instead, *see what really is!*

The Gospel is: Jesus has included us in His union with the Father and Spirit. It's all Him. Hear Jesus and live!

Since we are not separated, any ideas of how to 'get back to God' … won't work! And we eventually die of exhaustion or sadness, cynicism, despair, even though we have been faithful and true to 'the cause!' There is no pain greater than disappointed hope.

There is only one battle: union/separation.

There is a great difference between our (Western Evangelical) Jesus and the real Jesus!

Jesus's testimony always exposes darkness as darkness!

When we cannot see what is, we don't know who we are!

The light of Christ in us shines in *The Great Darkness—the assumption of separation.*

Jesus stacked the deck with inclusion of everything!

Pastor Don Keathley said, "As the world of religion continues to fall apart a bigger world of grace and love is being revealed that will swallow up everything contrary to the nature of our Father."

Jesus's "I Am" Trumps Evil's "I Am Not"

In *Patmos*, Baxter Kruger wrote: *Prayer is listening to Jesus and sharing your heart with Him. He will tell you what He is doing and as soon as He does, you act on what He says! We get the water ... He changes it to wine. Like Jesus with His Father, we share in what Jesus is doing. He is the Lord of all things: Victorious Lamb, Father's Son, Creator, Anointed One, and He refuses to live His life without us!*

Jesus's 'I Am' always trumps Ophis's 'I am not.'

From victory to victory the Lamb leads!

Pretending eventually leads to despair. Striving always leads to exhaustion!

The Holy Spirit turns our sorrow into eyes to behold Jesus!

Jesus appears in our darkness!

Shame is Ophis' crop dusting.

Jesus is in the real us.... with our shame, condemnation and darkness. He is never ashamed of us. Neither is Papa or Sarayu!

We can never discover Jesus inside our darkness and never know His union with the real us or His Father's love while we refuse to acknowledge our darkness. We pretend, hide, medicate, seek salvation in our heads and create an external religion. We conjure up scapegoats to blame for our own misery... even scapegoats within us!

When Ophis attacks, he is attempting to get me to feel his own evil conscious as my own conscious. Lies and accusations are all that he has to fight with. Remember, Jesus who is Face to Face with the Father, is in me! Turn to Him and receive affirmation! Never shame!

Jesus has given you His own eyes... hold no secrets from Him and you will see everything with His eyes!

The broken me is the ME JESUS IS IN! He became sarx (NT Greek: 'flesh'). He is with me in my darkness!

Jesus was in the beginning face-to-face with the Father ... out of God's being. Now He is also in us – in our darkness. That is the gospel!

Inseparable Union

Ephesians 5:31–33 says, "For this reason a man shall leave his father and mother and be joined to his wife, and the two shall become one flesh." This is a great mystery, but I speak concerning Christ and the church. Nevertheless let each one of you in particular so love his own wife as himself, and let the wife *see* that she respects *her* husband."

(MIRROR) (verse 32): "The secret of a successful marriage is reflected in this inseparable union between Christ and the church, as God's redeemed image and likeness in mankind. (This union ultimately defines both marriage and church.)"

Our marriage relationship is a mystery, like Christ and His church; however, now we can start *seeing what really is*, and it's no longer a mystery!

As Paul wrote in Romans 5, our old "husband, Mr. Law," died, and we no longer have any relationship to him. Jesus initiated, drew us all into Him and made us His bride. We have His name, identity, inheritance. We have all that He is … for better or worse, rich or poor, sickness and health, and nothing will ever separate us from His love!

That is who we are … our true identity … and Jesus did that! He chose us, and He transferred us from the kingdom of darkness into His Kingdom of light. He made us pure, spotless, His perfect bride! Now, just like any bride that has a former identity, we grow into learning who we are and realize the rights and privileges of being His bride!

Jesus wants you to know that you are His beloved Bride!

Pastor Don Keathley said, "The good news is that the Father through the Son in the Spirit has already chosen, redeemed, justified, sanctified, fully reconciled, forgiven, made righteous and made you complete in Christ. All of this was done in Christ before the foundation of the world… Now you be reconciled or in simple English, wake up to who you really are and live the abundant life that He promised in the here and now."

Steve McVey: "The first thing God did after He created humans was that 'He blessed them.' That's who God is!"

Corrupt Communion

Think about your *ministry* … what God might be calling you to do or be. Many times, people long to have a *large* ministry and to *do important things* for God and His Kingdom.

However, consider, what ministry could ever be more important than a full-time Mom, a full-time Dad, a full-time spouse, a full-time friend?

Ephesians 4:29 (KJV): "Let no corrupt communication proceed out of your mouth, but that which is good to the use of edifying, that it may minister grace unto the hearers."

I love the above translation of this verse because it accurately (in my opinion) contrasts corrupt communication with grace. Corrupt communication would include the *lie of separation* and any teaching that God is angry at humanity, that there is separation between us and God, separation between 'the elect and the damned,' any hierarchy in the Kingdom, that God is vindictive, punitive, has to be appeased, is full of 'wrath' towards us, that we can gain and maintain a right relationship with God by our own efforts, etc. That is all corrupt and directly opposed to God's Grace!

Because of religion's pervasive teaching and influence, most of its adherents believe lies. So, where are people … especially children … to learn the truth about God's unconditional love, unconditional forgiveness, passion for community with us, amazing grace, acceptance, and inclusion … and the effects of Jesus's finished work at the cross?

The Holy Spirit of Christ seems to most often reveal these mysterious truths to us from another person whom we are in a relationship with and whom we trust. Many times, these truths are 'caught' as much as 'taught.' Many people who have never (fortunately) been a part of organized religion have a wonderful understanding of unconditional love, unconditional forgiveness, grace, acceptance, and inclusion because they have seen that in a parent, grandparent, spouse and/or friend!

We can impact the world in great ways for the Kingdom of

God simply by believing, teaching and modeling what the Trinity is really like to those in our little sphere of influence! That's what happened in the first church, and it thrived for about 300 years before religion began to corrupt it as the official state-required religion of Rome.

We have the great privilege and the very high calling of ministering grace to those in our lives who are in a position to see and hear just by watching and listening to us!

Jazz or Classical?

Jazz and jazz groups are many times loathed by 'religious' people and by 'play by the notes only' classically trained musicians. Jazz is free. Musicians aren't bound by notes on the page (the Law). Songs are never played exactly the same ... difference is encouraged! You'll hear many 'bad notes' from jazz musicians ... especially those who are learning and growing. But the 'bad notes' are incorporated into the song. No record is kept of them, and no one reminds the musicians of them (over and over).

Groups can vary tremendously in size and instrumentation. For our purposes, think of a sextet: piano, bass, drums, trumpet, sax, and trombone. Each has a different part to play and a different function. Each can have featured solos in a song ... or not. Not everyone plays all the time. Each has the creative freedom to do their thing within the parameters of the song as agreed upon by the group. Every part of the song is good in its own way. However, the song is arguably most powerful when the whole group is playing together and bringing the song to a climax.

All during a song the musicians themselves feel the music and feed off and inspire each other. The audience also is inspired by and feels the music. Listeners who aren't bound by traditional classical music standards (everything has to be done *the right way* every time—according to them) relate to, enjoy and literally become one with the music and musicians. Those who are bound by tradition and standards don't feel the music, don't relate but rather judge, evaluate, criticize, label and exclude 'them and us.'

Baxter Kruger said during a seminar in Lawrence, Kansas, that what church will be like is a jazz group with each individual member prepared. Then they come together to make music, and the Holy Spirit does something synergistically that no one expected, and it transcends all expectations and fills you with joy and you 'feel' it like you 'feel' the music!

2 Corinthians 3:6 (NLT): "God has enabled us to be ministers of His new covenant. This is a covenant not of written laws, but of the Spirit. The old written covenant ends in death; but under the

new covenant, the Spirit gives life."

(MIRROR): "It is God's signature in our spirit that authorizes New Testament ministry. We are not qualified by a legal document endorsed by a fellow human. The letter (of the law) is the administration of death; it is the Spirit (of grace) that quickens life."

Where the Spirit is, there is life and freedom! *Seeing what really is* with Jesus' eyes leads to life abounding!

Papa's Affirmation To You

When you start *seeing what really is*, you will often hear Papa say to you words like:

"I am completely Good!"

"I totally love you ... and everyone ... unconditionally!"

"I have done My finished work for everyone!"

"I have and continue to pour out and lavish My undeserved unmerited grace on all people ... without exception!"

"I have reconciled and included everyone to me ... without limits!"

"I am in everyone and one with everyone ... with no exceptions; no one is excluded!"

"I am for you ... and everyone!"

That's who God is! He has always been in you and with you in every single second ... in your darkness and shame, and in your joy. He has always been in and with you ... you have never been separated. Can you see now that there has never been any shame or condemnation or disappointment or loathing on His part?

Those are all lies from the assumption of separation. They only exist in the *darkness*. You have been transferred from the Kingdom of darkness into Christ's Kingdom of light. You see now that Papa, Jesus, Sarayu ... who are love, have always been in you and with you.

That means that you are incredibly loved and valued! You have infinite value to God! You are Christ's pearl of great price! He sought you, found you, gave everything for you, saved you and hid you in Him. You are one with Christ!

Grace Is the Divine Music Of Life

Colossians 1:19 (MIRROR): "The great conductor of music will draw your life into the full volume of the harmony of the ages!"

Colossians 3:16 says, "Christ is the language of God's logic. Let His message sink into you with unlimited vocabulary, taking wisdom to the most complete conclusion. This makes your fellowship an environment of instruction in an atmosphere of music. Every lesson is a reminder, echoing in every song you sing, whether it be a psalm (raving about God in praise and worship accompanied by musical instruments) or a hymn (a testimony song) or a song in the spirit (a new spontaneous prophetic song). Grace fuels your heart with inspired music to the Lord!"

Colossians 4:6 says, "Season your conversation with grace. This remains the most attractive and appropriate option to respond in every situation."

Ephesians 4:29 says, "Let no corrupt communication proceed from your mouth but only that which edifies and builds up and ministers grace to those who listen!"

Zephaniah 3:17 says, " The LORD your God in your midst, The Mighty One, will save; He will rejoice over you with gladness, He will quiet *you* with His love, He will rejoice over you with singing."

God, who lavished all grace on you as a gift before creation, then manifested His grace for you in time and space at Jesus's finished work at the cross, and now continues to pour out His grace on you every second, literally rejoices over you with singing every minute!

Steve McVey posted on Facebook, "The cosmos pulsates with Divine Music. Those who believe hear and those who hear dance with their Creator to an ineffable song that transforms them like nothing else possibly could."

Something Happened

When I was 21, I joined the Kansas National Guard. I was a Private ... the lowest rank of all. I had no authority. Everyone else was over me. When I went to Basic Training, I was continually humiliated, harassed, embarrassed, shamed and yelled at. My superiors continually focused on my mistakes and shortcomings. I lived in fear. There were always consequences to my inadequacies. I was always being watched.

Then I went to Advanced Individual Training with the band at Ft. Leavenworth, Ks. I was a Private First Class ... not quite the lowest rank, but almost. I was a good trumpet player and was rewarded for that, but as the lowest ranking and newest member of the band, I was always scrutinized and was given all the 'punitive' assignments that no one else wanted. I was always fearful.

After that, I went home and was a member of the 42nd National Guard Band. Again, I was the lowest ranking person, was always watched, always fearful, always told what to do and had to defer to everyone else.

Then something happened!

Within a few short months, I was promoted and appointed Commanding Officer of the band. Because of the highest-ranking person in the Kansas National Guard's decision, I became ... instantly ... the Commanding Officer of the band. I had a bar pinned on my shoulder and became a Chief Warrant Officer.

Someone made a decision that in their opinion, I qualified to be an officer with all the responsibility, authority and perks thereof!

For a while, I didn't fully realize who I was or what my authority was. I still thought of myself as a private with no worth, no respect, who was always being told what to do. But gradually, I began to be confidently assured and started to understand that I was no longer a Private ... that person didn't exist. The old was gone. The new had come!

There was no longer any record of me being a Private ... I had a whole new identity! Nothing I had done as a Private mattered! My past had absolutely no bearing on who I now was!

2 Corinthians 5:17 (MIRROR): "Now, in the light of your co-inclusion in Jesus death and resurrection, whoever you thought you were before, in Christ you are a brand-new person! The old ways of seeing yourself and everyone else are over. Acquaint yourself with the new!"

Your New Standing Negates Your Past

For a while, I had been a private in the United States Army National Guard. During that time, I made a lot of mistakes, some intentional and some not. Did those things actually 'happen to me' before? Of course … but they were no longer a reality. Once I was made an officer, I had a whole new identity … a whole new standing with the army and with my fellow bandsmen and women. I had a new standing that totally negated my past. I no longer wore the uniform of a private. I was now a Commanding Officer.

That's a great picture of our past and what Jesus accomplished for us at the cross. He took away the old us, and it died with Him. When He rose from the dead, we rose with Him in our totally new identity. The old is gone, and the new is here!

Once I started to realize who I was in my new identity, I held my head higher, and I stood up straighter. I no longer worried that I was going to be yelled at by drill sergeants who were trying to verbally beat me into submission. I no longer lived in military fear! I was no longer called Private (and much worse!). I was now addressed as 'Chief,' 'Sir,' or 'Mister.' I still had my old Private uniform in the closet. It was totally different than an Officer's uniform. They were unmistakably different! If I wanted to, I could put my old Private uniform on, think like and live like a Private … but I would be unnecessarily living a lie. That wasn't me. The person who was a Private was gone.

We each have that option now as new Creations in Christ. We can choose to wear our old uniform fashioned by the lies of separation, exclusion, not measuring up, at odds with God, etc., if we want to. And occasionally, I find myself doing that. However, the Holy Spirit of Christ always gently reminds me that's not who I really am!

Romans 13:14 (NASB): "But put on the Lord Jesus Christ, and make no provision for the flesh in regard to *its* lusts."

Galatians 3:27 says, "Whoever is immersed in Christ is fully clothed with Him! He is your brand-new wardrobe confirming your sonship!"

Colossians 3:1 (NASB): "[*Put on the New Self*] Therefore if you have been raised up with Christ, keep seeking the things above, where Christ is, seated at the right hand of God." (MIRROR): "See yourselves co-raised with Christ! Now ponder with persuasion the consequences of your co-inclusion in Him. Relocate yourselves mentally! Engage your thoughts with throne room realities where you are co-seated in the executive authority of God's right hand."

You Are Already In

As you learn to hear His voice and abide (dwell in seamless union with) in Him, He will continually reveal greater depths of this truth of union with Him as contrasted with *The Lie of Separation*.

This Truth ... Christ in you ... will set you free from trying to get back in God's good graces, trying to get 'in,' because you will know The Truth that you are *already in*!

You will then be able to experience and enjoy a new and better way of living ... New Life in Christ. You will be:

- Free from feeling like you have to perform to please God.
- Free from fear, doubt, and anxiety.
- Free from fear of being punished by an angry God.
- Free from guilt, condemnation, and shame.
- Free from fear of death.
- Free from wondering which denomination or doctrine is 'right.'
- Free from 'God's Judgment.'
- Free from judging others.
- Free from excluding others.
- Free to enjoy life.
- Free to love.

In this new and better way of living, every day you find out that God is better than you thought the day before!

Pastor Don Keathley said, "A free gift *is not* I will give you but *you must*... A free gift *is not* I will give if *you will first*... A free gift *is not* I will give *when you*... A gift that has strings or stipulations and conditions is not a gift... a real free gift is a one-way act of love without regard to how the recipient uses or does not use the gift to its full advantage...everything that the father has given to his creation has been in the form of a free gift."

It Looks Like 'Unconditional Love' And 'Rest'

So … how can you tell that you are *seeing what really is?*

What will your life look like? How will you feel? What will be your prevailing mindset?

Will other people notice any difference in you? Will it be a good difference, or will they label you a religious wacko and distance themselves from you? Will your speech sound like you've swallowed the communion table, and will every other word you say end in eth?

Will you have to give up everything you enjoy and spend all your time doing dreary, unfulfilling ministry things?

Will you need to no longer hang out with old friends whom you love and enjoy because they aren't Christians?

If you answered 'yes' to that last set of questions, may I respectfully ask you to read this book again?

Here's what your life will look like—it will be characterized by unconditional love for everyone, joy, peace, patience, kindness, goodness, gentleness, faith, under control, mercy, compassion, and grace for everyone. You will find yourself truly enjoying life … and people. And … your life will look like REST. Jesus seems to put a very high premium on rest!

Pastor Don Keathley wrote, "We must accept the fact that grace is revealed layer upon layer. With that in mind we have to give each other grace for where we are in going through those layers. Just because someone is waaaaay back where you were last year does not mean they are still in bondage and if someone is way out there past where you can see where grace could ever take us does not make them a heretic … Plenty of room in grace, which is THE ONE THING we all need no matter where we walk."

Matthew 11:28–30 (MSG): "Are you tired? Worn out? Burned out on religion? Come to me. Get away with me and you'll recover your life. I'll show you how to take a real rest. Walk with me and work with me— watch how I do it. Learn the unforced rhythms of grace. I won't lay anything heavy or ill-fitting on you. Keep company with me and you'll learn to live freely and lightly."

Francois Du Toit writes in his commentary on Hebrews 3:19, "The ultimate proof of faith is not experience of the supernatural, but entering into His rest. His rest celebrates His perfect work. He longs for you to discover your own completeness and perfection as seen from His point of view. His rest is sustained in you by what he sees, knows and says about you in reference to the finished work of Christ. Jesus is what God believes about you!"

The Faith Of Jesus

The following is from chapter 18 of *Patmos* by Baxter Kruger:

"The first faith of all is the faith of Jesus. As Jesus reveals Himself in us, He is sharing Himself, His eyes, His faith with us. Do you see? From His eyes to ours, from faith to faith.

"Jesus calls us to a change of the way we see His Father first, then ourselves and others, until we believe what He believes.

"Without Jesus you would only have what you do and do not see—imprisoned by your feelings, or lack of them, lost in your head. As we discover Jesus in us, we are given a way to change our minds and our feelings. With our 'Amen' to Jesus comes freedom to live from His 'I Am' from the heart.

"Living from Jesus' faith, from his 'I Am' gives us confidence to turn toward our Father. When we see the Father through Jesus' eyes, we experience life– eternal life.

"'*Educare*'– drawing out that which is within. The knowing, His knowing, His believing, His 'I Am,' is deeper in us than our own thinking and challenges our thoughts to expand. He calls us to hear Him and say, 'Amen' to Him, and to live out of His life within us. We take sides with Him against the way we see.

"Jesus's 'I Am' is His code phrase for Jesus Himself and the way He sees and believes, and all that Jesus is in His faith and faithfulness, victory and love, confidence and freedom, joy and life and communion with His Father in the Holy Spirit— eternal life."

The following is from Chapter 25:

"Oneness, the womb of the creation of all things. The Father is in the Son, the Son in the Father, and the Holy Spirit in the Father and the Son. It has always been so and always will be. And we … every broken fragment, are in the Son and He in us. All will see, 'In that day you will know that I am in My Father, and you in Me, and I in you.'"

Keys To Understanding What Really Is

"Seven keys to Seeing What Really Is, by Pastor Don Keathley.
1. Seeing that we are new creations!
2. Seeing that we live out of God's favor, not our good works!
3. Knowing and being convinced that the Kingdom of God has supplied you with all you need!
4. Knowing that God speaks to us continually!
5. Knowing that God's grace is working in everyone!
6. Daily being mindful of God's Omnipresence!
7. Knowing that you receive Grace with God's measure (and it's bigger than you can ever comprehend!)

"Faith is being totally persuaded that God is persuaded about you!

"You've got a personal optometrist and His name is Dr. Jesus–He's helping you see what really is!"

Romans 12:1–2 (MSG) (Italics mine): "So here's what I want you to do, God helping you: Take your everyday, ordinary life—your sleeping, eating, going-to-work, and walking-around life—and place it before God as an offering. Embracing what God does for you is the best thing you can do for him. Don't become so well-adjusted to your culture that you fit into it without even thinking. Instead, *fix your attention on God.* You'll be changed from the inside out. Readily recognize what He wants from you, and quickly respond to it. Unlike the culture around you, always dragging you down to its level of immaturity, God brings the best out of you, develops well-formed maturity in you."

Objective and Subjective

Objectively, we are one with the Trinity. Subjectively, many of us are not yet aware of that truth. The following verses help us start to grasp our identity of union and oneness (parentheses comments added by me):

1 Corinthians 6:17 (MIRROR): "In our union with Him, we are one spirit with the Lord."

1 Corinthians 12:13 (NLT) (Parenthesis mine) (Subjectively in the temporary, seen realm): "Some of us are Jews, some are Gentiles, some are slaves, and some are free. But (Objectively) we have all been baptized into one body by one Spirit, and we all share the same Spirit."

1 John 5:20 (NASB): "And we know that the Son of God has come, and has given us understanding so that we may know Him who is true; and we are in Him who is true, in His Son Jesus Christ. This is the true God and eternal life."

John 14:9–11 says, "Jesus said to him, 'Have I been with you so long, and yet you have not known Me, Philip? He who has seen Me has seen the Father; so how can you say, "Show us the Father"? Do you not believe that I am in the Father, and the Father in Me? The words that I speak to you I do not speak on My own *authority*; but the Father who dwells in Me does the works. Believe Me that I *am* in the Father and the Father in Me, or else believe Me for the sake of the works themselves.'"

John 10:30 (NLT): "The Father and I are one."

John 14:10–11, 26 (NIV): "Don't you believe that I am in the Father, and that the Father is in me? The words I say to you I do not speak on my own authority. Rather, it is the Father, living in me, who is doing His work. Believe me when I say that I am in the Father and the Father is in me; the Advocate, the Holy Spirit, whom the Father will send in my name, will teach you all things and will remind you of everything I have said to you."

Romans 12:5 (Italics and parenthesis mine): "We, *being* many (Subjectively), are one body in Christ (Objectively), and individually members of one another."

Taking Sides with Jesus

Seeing what really is … means asking Jesus to show you what He sees and taking sides with Him!

There is only one question—union or separation. If there is separation, then there are countless questions, bogus answers, denominations, doctrines and 'ways to get back to God.'

If you believe the *lie of separation*, you will see separation in scripture, separation in your concept of God, separation in your relating to God, and separation in your evaluation (judging) of other people. Separation everywhere. You will remain in the same spiritual darkness that Adam and Eve entered into when they believed the lie that they were separated. As a result, they could no longer *see what really is.*

God still loved them unconditionally … but they couldn't see that.

God still came to them in love and grace … but they couldn't see that.

God still wanted to relate to them in love and grace … but they couldn't see that.

They were still right with God … nothing had changed in their relationship as far as God was concerned … but they couldn't see that.

God was not angry with them … but they couldn't see that.

God did not demand sacrifices and have to be appeased … but they couldn't see that.

They did not have to work to get right with God … but they couldn't see that. God still delighted in them … but they couldn't see that. They were still made in the image and likeness of God … but they couldn't see that.

God didn't count their sins against them … but they couldn't see that. God wasn't repulsed by their sins … but they couldn't see that. The assumption of separation *is* the *great darkness.*

Seeing what really is completely hinges on our understanding the truth of *union* versus the *Lie of Separation.* As long as we believe in any sort of separation, we will not be able to fully *see what really is.*

Separation Thinking Keeps You In The Dark!

As long as we believe the lie that there's something—anything—a human must do to get right with God (even 'asking Jesus into your heart' or 'confessing your sins and asking for forgiveness'), we believe *The Lie of Separation*, and we won't be able to *see what really is.*

The world, under the influence of the 'ruler of this world,' continually repeats The *Lie of Separation*. 'Worldly thinking' is actually 'separation thinking!'

The major, overriding issue of ALL time for ALL mankind is seeing only *union* and rejecting any notion of separation.

When you realize that Jesus is in everyone and speaks to everyone, you realize that the Holy Spirit of Christ communicates even to people who have never heard of Jesus, don't believe in Jesus or have 'rejected' Jesus.

In the episode of *Hour of Power* hosted by Dr. Robert Schuller that aired on May 31st, 1997, Billy Graham said, "What God is doing today is calling people out of the world for His name. Whether they come from the Muslim world, or the Buddhist world, or the Christian world, or the non-believing world, they are members of the body of Christ because they've been called by God. They may not even know the name of Jesus, but they know in their hearts they need something that they don't have and they turn to the only light they have and I think they're saved and they're going to be with us in heaven."

Everything good comes from God. So, when we observe a person who *appears* to be far from God doing something good, we can see what really is: That's Jesus doing something good through and as them—whether they know it's Him or not!

Once we understand and believe *union*, that understanding actually eliminates all religion, cults, denominations, and doctrines. It puts them all out of business (which is why they resist and fight so hard against God's inclusion of all).

Once we are convinced that Jesus actually did finish His work, then we start to know as we have always been known and start to *see what really is!*

Union vs. separation is the lens for:

- Reading scripture
- Relationships
- Worship
- Service
- Love
- Everything!

Union is what really is. Union is love and grace in action! Worship is love responding to Love!

'Hell' Comes From The Great Darkness

The pagan concept of hell being a place where an angry god demands human sacrifice and punishment to appease it and fulfill its desire for revenge is a lie that religion has bought into hook, line and sinker ... from *the great darkness.*

Hell is believing in separation. When you believe that you or anyone can be separated from God, you believe that separated condition—in this life or the life-after—is 'hell.'

The assumption of separation is the *great darkness* that prevents us from *seeing what really is.*

Religion has deceived many of us into believing the obvious contradiction that God is Good and God is for us ... yet He must punish forever those who disagree with Him. We know that we, and very few other humans, would even want to torture someone for all eternity just because they disagreed with us. Yet we've bought the lie that God, who is good, can do just that and *still* be good. No one really wants to get close to or have a personal relationship with a being like that.

Believing that God can be good and God can be love ... and still do evil, especially by punishing people in 'hell' forever, causes a cognitive dissonance in people. Most eventually check out, leave the church and leave organized religion. When religion teaches 'separation' and an 'angry god,' many people decide to not have anything to do with that 'god.' It's not Jesus's Papa, The Only True God, whom they are rejecting! They are rejecting the fictitious 'god' of religion. Ironically, they are the ones who are right in rejecting that 'god.'

'Hell' is any belief that God's plan for certain people is eternal separation. That belief is a lie and is totally contrary to God's Good News of Grace for everyone. Believe God.

Embracing Union

Seeing what really is means no longer believing in separation and instead embracing UNION!

The apostle Paul went to great lengths to assure us that separation is impossible!

Romans 8:31–39 (MIRROR): "All these things point to one conclusion; God is for us! Who can prevail against us? The gift of His son is the irrefutable evidence of God's heart towards us. He held nothing in reserve; but freely and undeservedly gave everything we could ever wish to have; this is what our joint sonship is all about.

"God has identified us, who can disqualify us? His word is our origin. No one can point a finger; He declared our innocence. What further ground can there possibly be to condemn man? In His death, He faced our judgment; in His resurrection, He declares our innocence; the implications cannot be undone! He now occupies the highest seat of authority as the executive of our redemption in the throne room of God.

"What will it take to distance us from the love of Christ? You name any potential calamity: intense pressure of the worst possible kind, cluster-phobia, persecution, destitution, loneliness, extreme exposure, life-threatening danger, or war?

"On the contrary, in the thick of these things our triumph remains beyond dispute. His love has placed us above the reach of any onslaught. This is my conviction, no threat whether it be in death or life; be it angelic beings, demon powers or political principalities, nothing known to us at this time, or even in the unknown future; no dimension of any calculation in time or space, nor any device yet to be invented, has what it takes to separate us from the love of God demonstrated in Christ. Jesus is our ultimate authority."

Mature Spirituality

Richard Rohr wrote in an article titled *Mature Spirituality*, "We cannot *attain* the presence of God because we're already totally in the presence of God. What's absent is awareness. Little do we realize that God is maintaining us in existence with every breath we take. Each time you take another breath, realize that God is choosing you again and again—and yet again (Ephesians 1:4, 9–11). We have nothing to work up to or even learn. We do, however, need to unlearn some things, and most especially we must let go of any thought that we have ever been separate from God.

"To become aware of God's presence in our lives, we have to accept what is often difficult, particularly for people in what appears to be a success-driven culture. We have to accept that human culture is in a mass hypnotic trance. Plato already said this, as most religions do at the higher levels. We are sleep-walkers, 'seeing through a glass darkly' (1 Corinthians 13:12). Wisdom teachers from many traditions have recognized that we human beings do not naturally see; *we have to be taught how to see.* That's what religion is for, to *help us let go of illusions and pretenses so we can be more and more present to what actually is.*

"We have to learn to see what is already here. Such a simple directive is hard for us to understand. We want to *attain* some concrete information or *achieve* an improved morality or *learn* some behavior that will make us into superior beings. We have a 'merit badge' mentality. We worship success. We believe that we get what we deserve, what we work hard for, and what we are worthy of. It's hard for Western people to think in any other way. But any expectation of merit or reward actually keeps us from the transformative experience called grace.

"Experiencing radical grace is like living in a different world. It's not a world in which I labor to get God to notice me and like me or where I strive for spiritual success. It's not a cosmic game of crime and punishment. God cannot be seen through such a small and dirty lens."

The Truth Of All Truths Is Union

You, and all of mankind, are not only in God's family, not only unconditionally loved and forgiven by God, not only totally right with God because of His grace and not only totally accepted and included in His family because of what they have already done for you. As great as those things are, The Truth of all Truths is even better!

You are *ONE* with Papa, Jesus, and The Holy Spirit. You are *UNITED*! We are all in total *UNION*! Christ is in you, and you are in Christ. You cannot get any closer to God, and you can never be less close to God! They have made it so!

That's different than just having a relationship with God. That's different from being friends with God. That's different from believing in God. You are in Union with God—One with God—you are the Bride of Christ!

The *great lie of darkness* continually lies to you and says none of this is true. It lies and says you are separated. It condemns, shames and guilts you. It deceives you into believing that it's your fault that you are separated from God and there's something you must do to get back to being with God. When you do some of the things it deceives you into doing, then you feel pride, that by your effort, you got closer to God.

Any and all striving and doing to try to please God, get right with God, merit God's favor … is *TOTALLY WORTHLESS* and *USELESS* and *COUNTER-PRODUCTIVE*! You cannot earn, merit or achieve what you already have! You can't get to where you already ARE!

Jesus told you in John 14:20, "In that day you will know that just as I am in My Father, you are in Me and I am in you!"

That *day* came at the culmination of His finished work at the cross where God included everyone *IN CHRIST*!

There is *NO SEPARATION* … there is only *UNION*! That *UNION* was brought about by God in Jesus's Finished Work at the Cross.

2 Corinthians 5:17 says, "In Christ, you are a brand-new per-

son! The old ways of seeing yourself and everyone else are over. Acquaint yourself with the new!" See what really is!

See To It That No One Takes You Captive

We can be prevented from *seeing what really is* by the Darkness's deception.

Colossians 2:9–11 says, "See to it that no one takes you captive through philosophy and empty deception, according to the tradition of men, according to the elementary principles of the world, rather than according to Christ. For in Him all the fullness of Deity dwells in bodily form, and in Him you have been made complete, and He is the head over all rule and authority."

Colossians 1:13–14 says, "God has delivered us from the power of darkness and conveyed *us* into the kingdom of the Son of His love, in whom we have redemption through His blood, the forgiveness of sins."

We have been delivered from the power of the darkness of our minds, but we can still go there. It has no power over us—unless we give it power. It's not real … it just feels real.

The following is from *Patmos*, by Baxter Kruger:

If we believe in the lie of darkness and separation, then we believe that we have to figure out how to get right with God. So we invent something in our mind and pursue it to bring freedom.

Then we die of exhaustion because it can't work. We aren't separated to begin with!

If we believe that we are separated from God and have to find our way back, we are open to anyone's claim for how to get there– but nothing will work!

We all die of exhaustion, sadness, cynicism and despair … even those of us who have been faithful and 'true to the cause.'

'Worldly thinking' means 'thinking separation!'

If you believe that you are separated from Jesus, all you have is your own 'faith.'

Such separation only exists in our imagination – where 'our faith' is.

There is really only one faith!

We have terribly underestimated Jesus! Everything is about Him! He is the creator of everything!

JESUS IS GRACE AND LIFE PERSONIFIED!

Jesus, who is Grace and Life personified, lives in us. He has given us His glory, and His Holy Spirit continually assures us that The Father loves us just as He loves Jesus … and always has since before creation. The Holy Spirit continually reveals and reminds us that we are One with Jesus and the Father!

John 14:20 (Jesus): "At that day you will know that I am in My Father, and you in Me, and I in you."

John 17:3 (Jesus): "And this is eternal life, that they may know You, the only true God, and Jesus Christ whom You have sent."

John 17:13 says, "But now I come to You, and these things I speak in the world, that they may have My joy fulfilled in themselves."

John 17:20–26 says, "I do not pray for these alone, but also for those who will believe in Me through their word; that they all may be one, as You, Father, are in Me, and I in You; that they also may be one in Us, that the world may believe that You sent me. And the glory which You gave me I have given them, that they may be one just as We are one: I in them, and You in Me; that they maybe be made perfect in one, and that the world may know that You have sent me and have loved them as you have loved Me. Father, I desire that they also whom You gave Me may be with Me where I am, that they may behold My glory which You have given Me; for You have loved Me before the foundation of the world. O righteous Father! The world has not known You, but I have known You; and these have known that You sent Me. And I have made Your name known to them, and will make it known to them, that the love with which You loved me may be in them, and I in them."

Colossians 1:27 says, "This is the mystery: Christ in you, the hope of glory!"

Since Grace is God's (who IS pure, unconditional agape love that always does what is best for the other) unconditional love, NOTHING IMPURE can come from what is pure!

Therefore, everything God says and thinks and does flows from His pure love. Therefore:

- 'wrath' must be something that benefits us … it IS 'orge,' a strong, violent, passionate display of love FOR us that would also be AGAINST anything that hurts us (sin). 'Wrath' cannot be something vindictive that punishes us.
- 'Punishment' must be something good for us. It IS purifying, not punitive.
- 'Hate' cannot be as we have been taught. It can't be 'hate of us'—it must be 'hate' of anything that hurts us.

What we believe about God's essence, His nature, colors everything we think about God and how we interpret scripture. Greek, the original New Testament language, often has many different meanings of a single word—and sometimes they are contradictory. Therefore, translators are going to choose whatever meaning fits with their concept of God's essence, nature, and actions. Thus, the Greek word 'orge'—any violent expression of emotion—which could be love, joy, anger, etc., may be translated 'wrath' or 'love' or 'joy' or 'anger.'

You'll find those who believe in Eternal Conscious Torment translating 'orge' as 'wrath,' and you'll find those who believe in Eternal Conscious Unconditional Love translating 'orge' as God's "white-hot consuming fiery love that burns away all impurities and leaves only the pure!"

In a similar fashion, the Greek word 'pas' means 'all.' Those who believe that God loves ALL, He is for ALL, ALL were included in Christ's finished work at the cross, Christ is in ALL, for ALL and through ALL and Christ is the Savior of ALL, believe that 'pas' means 'all.' Those who believe that mankind is separated from God and has to do something, make some transaction happen to get God to forgive and include them, believe that 'pas' means only 'some of all groups,' i.e., 'some' Jews, 'some' Gentiles, etc.

Those who believe that the Grace of God is for all, take heart in these verses:
- "For the grace of God has appeared, bringing salvation to all men" (Titus 2:11).
- "… we have fixed our hope on the living God, who is

the Savior of all men, especially of believers" (1 Timothy 4:10).

- "God saved us and called us with a holy calling, not according to our works, but according to His own purpose and grace which was given to us in Christ Jesus before time began, but has now been revealed by the appearing of our Savior Jesus Christ, who has abolished death and brought life and immortality to light through the gospel" (2 Timothy 1:9–10).
- "Jesus is the atoning sacrifice for our sins, and not only for ours but also for the sins of the whole world" (1 John 2:2).
- "Jesus was the true Light which, coming into the world, enlightens every man" (John 1:9).
- "By God's will we have been sanctified through the offering of the body of Jesus Christ once for all" (Hebrews 10:10).
- "Jesus offered one sacrifice for sins for all time" (Hebrews 10:12).
- "God (The Father) was in Christ (at the cross) reconciling the entire cosmos to Himself, not counting anyone's sins against them and He has given us the ministry of reconciliation!" (2 Corinthians 5:19)

THE THRONE OF GRACE HAS SPECIAL MEANING FOR US!

Hebrews 4:16 says, "Let us then approach God's throne of grace with confidence, so that we may receive mercy and find grace to help us in our time of need."

What is the Throne of God like? It is THE THRONE OF GRACE!

It is IN us! We are the Temple—the dwelling place of God! 1 Corinthians 3:16 says, "Do you not know that you are the temple of God and that the Spirit of God dwells in you?"

The THRONE OF GOD IS IN YOU! Jesus, Papa, and the Holy Spirit are all IN YOU!

We go to Christ in us, the hope of glory, to obtain mercy and find GRACE to help us in time of need!

1. There is NO 'bad' judgment throne of God. There is only the THRONE OF GRACE where we are reminded and assured daily that we have already been judged and made right, forgiven, justified, sanctified, purified, included and accepted into the Divine Triune Circle Dance of God's Unconditional love and all that flows from it! All our sins have been taken away!

2. To say that God is on His mercy seat, the THRONE OF GRACE, *now*, but "one day he will get off it and go to a great white judgment throne and change his disposition totally and no longer be love and grace, but instead be wrath and judgment" ... is to disparage God's nature and character and is to totally misunderstand His unconditional love that never fails!

With this revealed understanding of John 17, you can actually change the world!

Jesus prayed for His disciples and for us: "Father, I pray that they all may be one, as You, Father, are in Me, and I in You; that they also may be one in Us, that the world may believe that You sent Me ... And the glory which You gave Me I have given them ... (God's glory is His Grace!) that they may be one just as We are one: I in them, and You in Me … that they may be made perfect in one … and that the world may know that You have sent Me, and have loved them as You have loved Me."

Jesus Gave us His glory …which is His Grace—AND … told us that The Father loves us just like He loves Jesus and has since before creation!

Can you imagine that?

God's glory is His grace—there is only One God … and no other fictitious god that humans have ever imagined … has ever said to have had grace … or to be grace … or to give grace.

Every single other imagined god had to be appeased in some way to get that imaginary god to bless people. You had to sacrifice—even your own kids! You had to do rituals—sometimes with bloodletting. You had to give—a lot. You had to believe exactly right … maybe then you could get that god to bless you.

But not the only true God … Jesus' Papa. His glory, what makes Him glorious, what sets Him apart, is His grace!

And He has given us His grace—which means not only do we have all the continuing benefits of His grace, but we have grace upon grace, way more than we can ever use—we have an unlimited supply of grace—to do what with …?

To give to others! And not just little bits here and there when they ask for it—NO! We have an unlimited supply of God's glory—His grace—in us—to give to everyone else.

How do people know that you're a child of God? Not by what you believe—not by your reading the bible or going to church or serving at the homeless center. Not by what you don't do (drink, smoke, gamble, cuss, etc.).

The way people know you are God's child, the way they see Christ in you … the hope of glory … is for them to see you lavishing grace on everyone all the time! Because that's what Jesus does!!!

And get this: The Father loves us just like He loves Jesus and has since before creation! Grace is God's unconditional love in perpetual action!

Think about that, think about Jesus Christ—the Son of God—the Savior of the World—God Himself—think about how the Father must love Him—and Jesus says that The Father loves you JUST LIKE HE LOVES JESUS!

2 Tim 1:9–10 says, "God has saved us and called us with a holy calling, not according to our works, but according to His own purpose and grace which was given to us in Christ Jesus before time began, but has now been revealed by the appearing of our Savior Jesus Christ, who has abolished death and brought life and immortality to light through the gospel ..."

You have this magnificent, stupendous, stunning gift of all gifts—worth more than anything in the world gift—the gift of Grace—given to you by the only true God—who loves you just like He loves Jesus and gave you grace before creation.

Now, here's our practical application—here's what you and I can do to change other people's lives and literally change the world—one person at a time ...

We can give ... lavish ... grace on everyone we come in contact with!

It doesn't cost us anything. We don't have to learn or memorize anything. It's fun! It totally makes a difference in people's lives!

You and I can lavish grace on everyone we come in contact with—and what is the result? They will know that we're doing something supernatural—something from God. They will know we're Christ followers.

You know how you grow in grace? By giving it away!

And grace has NO 'but'... no conditions; it's just pure grace ... because God loves you like He does Jesus!

That's called Good News. That's what Grace Is!

About Paul Gray

Paul Gray is the author of the inspirational books *Convertible Conversations, Grace Is ..., Notes From Papa,* and *The Fish Net Experience.* He is a co-author of *Godly Men Make Godly Fathers.*

Paul's message, "Grace is *unconditional* love in action," focuses on helping people experience and enjoy God's love *without conditions* for all people. He has found that knowing God personally leads to enjoying and experiencing life at a much higher level!

He and his wife of 48 years, Kitsy, live in Lawrence, Kansas, where they continue to facilitate growing in grace at the church they founded in 1991, New Life in Christ. They have three wonderful grown children and six amazing grandchildren. *Convertible Conversations,* a short article series on a wide range of topics, are posted by Paul at ~~Online Community Church~~ on Facebook.

Paul's career began with his studies at the University of Kansas in 1965, where he formed his band, the Gaslite Gang, which made several national television performances and recorded five albums. They performed full-time from coast to coast for many years, doing educational concerts and clinics as well as performing at a variety of venues. Paul owned a variety of businesses, ranging from five retail music stores to a long-distance telephone company, as well as Paul Gray's Jazz Place, a popular Lawrence, Kansas, jazz venue where he performed with his group. Concurrently, he served in the United States Army National Guard and Army Reserves for 24 years as a bandmaster.

In 1999, his church started a medical clinic for homeless individuals, The Heartland Medical Clinic, where he was CEO for seven years. It continues to serve the medical needs of thousands of patients each year.

Paul Gray holds an education degree from the University of Kansas and a degree in Grace Theology from Global Grace Seminary.

His musical recordings, spiritual articles and videos can be found at www.gracewithpaulgray.com

Contact Information

Paul Gray, phone: 785.766.3624
Email: convertibleconversations@gmail.com
Website: www.gracewithpaulgray.com
Twitter: @chiefpaulgray

GRACE IS … ACTION STEPS

If you liked the spiritually liberating and emotionally healing message in *Grace Is …*, here are some ways you can help spread the GOOD NEWS message:

1. Write an Amazon review with a 5-star rating (if you think it is merited)

2. Send a copy of *Grace Is …* to your friends and family

3. Post a recommendation with the link on your Facebook page(s)

4. Start a home study discussing one chapter each week

5. Recommend Paul Gray for internet radio interviews

6. Watch and repost Grace With Paul Gray daily videos

7. Check out my other books and blogs at www.grace-withpaulgray.com

Explanation
(My Message and Assignment)

I very much relate to my namesake, the Apostle Paul, and can't improve on the Mirror version of Titus 1:1–3 (italics mine):

"Paul, the bondman of God, on assignment by Jesus Christ; my mission is to persuade people of their origin in God; by bringing them into a complete understanding of the truth as the only valid reference to meaningful devotion."

This is the life of the ages which was anticipated for generations; the life of our original design announced by the infallible resolve of God before time or space existed. (Mankind's union with God is the original thought that inspired creation … This was before the ages or any measure of calendar time existed, before the creation of the galaxies and constellations. There exists a greater dimension to eternity than what we are capable of defining within the confines of space and time! God's faith anticipated the exact moment of our redeemed union with Him for all eternity!) This life was made certain before eternal time. [BBE: 1949, Bible in Basic English]

My message announces the completeness of time; God's eternal moment realized the logic of our salvation. My message very much includes sharing what I've learned from wonderful teachers whom God has used greatly in unpacking *The Mystery of the Ages* (Christ in you, the hope of glory– Colossians 1:27). With their permission, I have quoted them rather extensively in *Grace Is ...* They include: Steve McVey, Baxter Kruger, Don Keathley, and William Paul Young.

In addition to these men listed above, I'm tremendously indebted to Francois du Toit, prolific author, speaker, teacher and translator of The Mirror Bible.

Through my studies and involvement with the Global Grace Seminary, I've been privileged to learn from a myriad of other great writers and teachers. My thinking is continually stretched and challenged by a number of people whom I read online every day.

There are many good English translations of the Bible. Unless otherwise noted, I have used the New King James Version because many people are somewhat acquainted with how it reads. Whenever possible, however, I use (and reference) the Mirror Word translation (© Copyright Francois du Toit 2016) because I feel it accurately represents Jesus, who is God's language and message to mankind.

As my friend Francois states, "There is no perfect translation, there is only a perfect Word: The Logic of God. The Bible is all about Jesus. What makes the book irresistibly relevant, is the fact that Jesus is all about you!"

I have attempted to correctly attribute quotes to their authors; however, I'm sure there are instances where I write something that has become so much of my understanding of the finished work of Christ that I'm not even aware how or through whom Papa first revealed it to me! Any such slights are certainly not intentional!

These men, as well as others, have helped me realize that there's more to what's going on in your life than meets the eye. There's an unseen spiritual dimension of life that is every bit as real as the visual world that we can discern by our five senses. God has given us all a '6th sense'—our spirit, which is where we hear from, see and relate to Him!

God's Spirit, the Holy Spirit of Christ who lives in us, communicates to us regularly. He reveals to us the truth about *what really is.* The things that we can see, hear, feel, touch and smell are all temporary. None of them last. They may be pleasant (or nasty), but they don't last.

It may appear to you that you're not a good person, or that God couldn't possibly like you or let alone want to be in your presence. It may appear to you that you could never be the kind of person that you really want to be. It may sound to you (from others' words) that you're a loser; no good; incompetent; not talented; not good looking; not _____ (you fill in the blank). But those things you see and hear are only temporary, and they aren't truth.

Jesus is Truth, and He is the Living Word of God ... that lasts forever. He says that God loves you unconditionally, is passionately obsessed with being with you every second, adores you, by His grace has already made everything right between you (and everyone) and Him, has totally accepted and included you in His family and reconciled you to Him forever!

True Truth, God's truth that lasts forever, says that Christ is living His life in you, as you and through you right now! God is working out all things for the good. God is for you and is with you and is taking care of you.

You can't see that via your five senses in the natural world. What you see, hear and feel in the world may very well contradict what God's truth says. So, God wants you to fix your eyes—focus—on what is true and real. You have to look with your spiritual eyes and hear with your spiritual ears … which God has graciously already given you.

Grace Is … is committed to helping you see with His eyes and hear with His ears!

2 Corinthians 4:18 says, "We do not look at the things which are seen, but at the things which are not seen. For the things which are seen *are* temporary, but the things which *are* not seen are eternal."

Books by Paul Gray

Convertible Conversations (~~available on Amazon~~)

#1 A Best Seller

Grace Is …

Notes From Papa (a 365-day devotional. book) is scheduled to be released in November 2018.

Fishnet Experience

Paul Gray is a co-author of *Godly Men Make Godly Fathers!* (15 Christian fathers have contributed to this book which was released in October 2017. Paul's chapter is titled "Parenting Help From THE Helper!" It is published by Motivation Champs Publishing.)

The above are available at A. com.

★ for Signed Copies ★

Bulk discount,

contact or at

CC@gml.m.

Paul Gray's Suggested Resources

Paul Gray's Top Ten Recommended Books
(In No Particular Order)

- *Patmos* by Baxter Kruger
- *Beyond an Angry God* by Steve McVey
- *God's Astounding Opinion of You* by Ralph Harris
- *The Shack* by William Paul Young
- *The Shack Revisited* by Baxter Kruger
- *Parable of the Dancing God* by C. Baxter Kruger
- *Saints in the Arms of a Happy God* by Jeff Turner
- *The Mirror Bible Paraphrase* by Francois Du Toit
- *Grace Walk* by Steve McVey
- *The Divine Dance* by Richard Rohr

Other Great Books

- By Andre Rabe
  Adventures in Christ
  The Secret of Contentment
  Metanoia
  Desire
  Imagine
- *It is Finished* by Blaise Foret
- By John Crowder
  Cosmos Reborn
  Mystical Union
- By Roy Richmond
  Simple Answers to What Seem to be Difficult Questions
- *Heavens Doors* by George. W. Sarris
- *The Unspoken Sermons* by George MacDonald
- By Wm. Paul Young
  Cross Roads
  Eve
  Lies We Believe About God
- *We Make the Road By Walking* by Brian D. McLaren

- *The Rest of the Gospel* by Dan Stone & Greg Smith
- By Bill Gillham
  What God Wishes Christians Knew About Christianity
  Lifetime Guarantee
- By Steve McVey
  The Secret of Grace
  Grace Rules
  52 Lies Heard in Church Every Sunday
  A Divine Invitation
  Unlock Your Bible
  When Wives Walk in Grace
- By Preston Gillham
  No Mercy
  Battle for the Round Tower
- *Helping Others Overcome Addiction* by Steve McVey & Mike Quarles
- *A Woman's Walk in Grace* by Catherine Martin
- *Bo's Café* by John Lynch, Bruce McNicol & Bill Thrall
- By C. Baxter Kruger
  The Great Dance
  God is For You
  Across All Worlds
  Jesus and the Undoing of Adam
- By John Eldredge
  Beautiful Outlaw
  Waking the Dead
- *He Loves Me!* by Wayne Jacobsen
- By Jody Marie White
  Chosen by God
  Scarlet White
- By Richard Rohr
  The Naked Now
  Falling Upward
  Everything Belongs
  Yes And
- By Peter Enns
  The Sin of Certainty

The Gospel in Ten Words
- *One Way Love* by Tullian Tchividjian
- *The Fish Net Experience* by Paul Gray
- *Been There, Done That* by Mike Miller
- *The Inescapable Love of God* by Thomas Talbott
- By Bradly Jersak
  A More Christlike God
  Her Gates Will Never Be Shut
- By Ivan A. Rogers
  Dropping Hell and Embracing Grace
  Grace Nuggets Uncovered
- By Brian Zahnd
  Unconditional
  Beauty Will Save The World
  Sinners in the Arms of a Loving God
  Farewell to Mars
- By Francois Du Toit
  God Believes in You
  The Logic of His Love
- By Kay Fairchild and Roy Richmond
  Living Out of Your Spiritual Resources Parts 1 and 2
  No Penal Substitution Parts 1 and 2

Devotional Books

- *The Grace Walk Devotional* by Steve McVey
- *Grace Walk Moments* by Steve McVey
- *Abba Calling* by Charles Slagle
- *Consuming Fire* by George MacDonald
- *My Utmost for His Highest* by Oswald Chambers
- *Jesus Calling* by Sarah Young

Recommended Grace Websites:

www.newlifeinchrist.com
www.perichoresis.com
www.gracewalk.org
www.donkeathley.com
www.gracewithpaulgray.com

Proof

Made in the USA
Columbia, SC
02 July 2018